To And

Islwyn

April 2003

SEEK FAIRER SKIES

Seek Fairer Skies
(Cais Loywach Nen)

by

ROY HUGHES

The Memoir Club

© Roy Hughes 2003

First published in 2003 by
The Memoir Club
Whitworth Hall
Spennymoor
County Durham

All rights reserved.
Unauthorised duplication
contravenes existing laws.

British Library Cataloguing in
Publication Data.
A catalogue record for this book
is available from the
British Library.

ISBN: 1 84104 026 6

Typeset by George Wishart & Associates, Whitley Bay.
Printed by Bookcraft (Bath) Ltd.

To my wife Marion, without whose diligent co-operation this book could not have been written.

Contents

Illustrations

Foreword

I HAVE KNOWN Roy Hughes for thirty years, as a close friend and as a wonderful colleague in Parliament. We are both from the same Monmouthshire mining stock – indeed, his family had lived in Blaenavon in my constituency of Torfaen. He served his Newport constituents diligently and loyally for three decades, and in 1997, was, rightly, elevated to the House of Lords as Lord Islwyn.

This book has been a labour of love. It charts the remarkable life of a working-class boy who, from his roots in the Sirhowy Valley, went to the Midlands to earn his living and to become a notable trade unionist and City Councillor for Coventry, and, from there, to return to his native South Wales to represent Newport in the House of Commons.

Chapter after chapter of this moving and deeply interesting book will reveal how Roy's interests have ranged from the local to the international. You will read of his deep commitment to the men and women of Newport; his passionate interest in and defence of the Welsh Steel Industry; his advocacy of the British Motor Industry, and of the rights of Trade Unionists; his activities on the international stage; and his Parliamentary battle for British Badgers. The book also tells of his great love for rugby, which he shared with my father on many occasions.

Roy has led a fabulously full and worthwhile life. This fine biography reveals a caring, committed and dedicated socialist, who, throughout his life, has been strengthened by his wife, his family and his friends, of whom I am privileged to be counted as one.

Paul Murphy, *MP for Torfaen and Secretary of State for Northern Ireland.*

CHAPTER 1

Early Days

PONTLLANFRAITH* is a village in the Sirhowy Valley in Wales
and this is the name given to the river running through it.
Sirhowy, the source of the river, is a small village just above
Tredegar in Gwent. Situated at the bottom of the valley where it
opens out, Pontllanfraith, with its two railway stations, provided
relatively easy access to most of South Wales and further afield.
It was here I was born in 1925 and a few months later there was
a major upheaval in my life for my father, a miner at nearby
Nine Mile Point Colliery, was on strike, which culminated in
the General Strike of 1926. My mother was expecting my sister
Megan at the time and so I was taken to my paternal
grandparents' home to be looked after but, in the event, I never
returned to my parents' home. It was a kind of Caucasian Chalk
Circle situation. This led to some minor difficulties between
the two branches of the family as I was 'piggy in the middle'
but, over the years, I maintained close and friendly contact with
all the family. My brother Granville is a close confidant, for in
early days we had so many shared experiences. My sister
Megan, a teacher, has lived in Malvern for many years. Her
husband David was a lecturer in Worcester Technical College.

My grandmother Hughes had died at a relatively young
age in 1917 but, living with my grandfather were his two
daughters Elizabeth and Hilda, together with his son, Ben. My
grandfather Hughes passed away in 1928. He had served in the
First World War, joining the Grenadier Guards and later

*Going back to 1492 the real name was Pont Llyn Fraith (literally Bridge end by the speckled pool) but it
changed in everyday speech to Pontllanfraith – hence the confusion sometimes about its meaning.

My sister Megan with her grandson David.

transferring to the Welsh Guards when they formed in 1917. He was wounded on the Somme. Earlier the family had lived in Blaenavon. My father and my aunts, Elizabeth and Hilda, were all born there. Originally, though, two Hughes brothers had migrated around 1850 from West Wales to Blaenavon, which was then a hive of industry.

When I was a small boy in the early 1930s I used to be taken up to Blaenavon by my Aunt Hilda to visit our many relatives there. Invariably I came home with a pocket full of coins, gifts from the various uncles and aunts we called on. Blaenavon was where the first industrialisation took place and there are many vestiges still to be seen of this industrial past. In 2001 Blaenavon was awarded World Heritage Status, alongside the Pyramids, the Taj Mahal and the Great Wall of China. Bearing in mind my family's close links with the town, this award was very pleasing to me.

Aunt Hilda.

There was no colliery in Pontllanfraith but it was sur-rounded by pits. When we were youngsters, the river was never referred to by its name, for it was always called the 'Black River'. Over the years, various collieries had deposited coal dust in it and it was truly as black as night. With the demise of the coal industry, the river has been restored to something like its natural beauty and is a haven for anglers.

Immediately after the war there was a fuel shortage and a lucrative trade grew up by the extraction of coal dust from the river for sale to local power stations. My mother's brother, Ray, who had just returned from the 14th Army in Burma, where he had been mentioned in despatches, was a prime instigator of this innovative activity. There was much money to be made, but the business was later taken over by a firm called Ryan's, who introduced sophisticated equipment for the extraction.

From early days my father's sister Elizabeth brought me up

Aunt Elizabeth outside 'our shop'.

and insisted that I attend Sunday School. First it was to Elim Baptist right opposite where we lived. I vaguely recall being put to stand on the seat (being too small) as revivalist hymns were sung. 'We marched upward to Zion...' as Mr Thomas pumped the organ. For some reason he was known locally as 'John Cow' but I never found out why. His son, Ray, a popular character in the village, was known as Hoggy Thomas. My mother's younger brother, Arthur, claimed to have given him this name when they were in school together in Pontllanfraith. My friends, however, tended to attend the Anglican Church Sunday School and I wished to go with them. My Aunt Elizabeth was quite ecumenical in her approach to religion and said, 'I don't care where you go so long as you go somewhere.' This ecumenical attitude, though, did not include Roman

Catholicism, which tended to be regarded as somewhat alien. There was, however, an RC Church near the top station (LMS, London Midland and Scottish) in Pontllanfraith. It was there that Sir Julian Hodge spent his early days. He had a cultured mother and I believe his father was a local engineer. Sir Julian later became a ticket collector at the bottom station (GWR, Great Western Railway) before embarking on his highly successful business career. Lady Hodge (Moira Thomas) came from Wyllie and I was very friendly with her brother Hugh during our school days. The children from Wyllie were brought to school by a special West Mon bus, as it was too far for them to go home at lunch time. Hugh Thomas came to our house with his sandwiches, which he ate with a cup of cocoa provided by Aunt Elizabeth.

Both she and her sister Hilda were quite enterprising in their way. In the early thirties a shop was opened in our front room. Toffee apples were a speciality and hordes of youngsters came to buy them during the school lunch hour. The toffee recipe is now in the House of Commons Food Book compiled by MPs. My Aunt Hilda made faggots and peas, which were sold hot and fresh on a Friday and there was a further sale on a Saturday morning. They were delicious. In later years Elizabeth branched out and, having passed a number of piano examinations earlier in life, undertook music lessons on the piano in the front room. She had a flourishing clientele amongst the local children. She was dedicated to the work and was not greatly concerned about the additional income it generated. Her charges were minimal.

At this time my Uncle Ben, who was a Griffin bus driver, married Edith James of Pentwynmawr. She worked for many years at Jones and Richards, the fashion store in Blackwood, and she was also the organist at New Bethel Congregational Church. They had three children, Glenys, John and David, and we all grew up together in Newbridge Road. Number 23

Cousin Glenys (Oliver).

became a sort of Victorian ménage, which accommodated various sections and generations of the family. I have always been very close to 'our Glenys', as I refer to her. One of her achievements was to teach me the words of 'Calon Lân'. A teacher, she settled in Wrexham with her husband, George. In adult life John achieved his ambition to become a garage proprietor. He is active in the Rotary movement and is a Rotary International Past President. Aided by his wife, Gertrude, John organised over the years the collection of medical supplies and obsolete hospital equipment which were very badly needed in Poland. This was at the time of the dissolution of the old USSR. Supplies were sent in convoys of lorries and John himself shared the driving. In 1995 he was awarded the Knight's Cross Order of Merit of the Polish Democratic Republic. It was a great pleasure for us to join John and his family at the Polish Embassy in London when he received his much-deserved honour. Meanwhile, my father, mother, brother and sister lived at the other end of the village.

In the early and mid thirties there was terrible industrial depression in South Wales. George V died in 1935 and his son, Edward VIII, came to the throne. The new monarch soon came to South Wales to see all the deprivation for himself. By now I was in the Church Lads Brigade and we were lined up on the Plough corner in Pontllanfraith as a sort of guard of honour for the King as he sped by in his car. He went on to Merthyr and there made his famous comment that 'something must be done'.

I passed the eleven plus examination but shortly after entering the local Grammar School★, I was struck down with diphtheria. In those days there were epidemics of this disease and occasionally children died. In my case I was sent to Aberbargoed Isolation Hospital, which was a tin-like building on the top of a mountain. I spent over four weeks there.

Even in those early days I was an avid newspaper reader and each day when I was in hospital the *Daily Herald* and the *Daily Mirror* were sent to me. They were, of course, both Labour newspapers. This reading was supplemented by the *Weekly Argus* so that I got the local news from childhood onwards. I was terribly interested in sport but soon, though, I turned from the back to the front pages of the newspapers and this, I feel sure, is what generated my interest in politics. Meanwhile, though, I was always anxious on a Saturday evening to get hold of the *Football Argus* for the results and reports of matches. Newport rugby was invariably featured on the front page and I recall the three-dimension score figures with tries and goal kicks recorded separately. The names of Walter Legge, Jack Knowles, Jim Hawkins and Albert Fear still come to mind.

In 1935 my Uncle Ben was teaching a neighbour, John Walker, to drive. His father kept a local shoe shop. One Saturday Cardiff was playing Swansea at the Arms Park and my

---

★The new school motto was 'Seek Fairer Skies'.

Uncle said, 'Let's go down to see Cliff Jones and Wooller.' I did not need a second invitation, so we set off in a little Austin Seven. On the Swansea side the scrum half was the great Haydn Tanner and he was partnered by Willie Davies who later went North. It was a memorable match.

One of my heroes was Tommy Farr, and I recall in 1937 getting up at 2.30 a.m. to listen to his great and courageous fight in America with Joe Louis for the world heavyweight title. We had what was then a 'posh' Murphy radio and, in the middle of the night and over fifteen bruising rounds, we were sustained with cups of tea and Welsh cakes.

In cricket, Glamorgan played Gloucestershire just before the war and, along with two school pals, Bertie Cripps and Morris Cole, I caught a train from the top station in Pontllanfraith to Newport, where we witnessed the great Walter Hammond make a century.

I took great pride in Newport County when they won promotion to the then Second Division just before the outbreak of war. To this day I can almost reel off the promotion team. The County has had a tragic history but I hope that before too long they will get back in the English League.

The Headmaster of our school, Mr David Bowen, was a harsh disciplinarian and I often wonder how he would have fared today. A favourite memory relating to the school is of the teacher, Mr Edgar Phillips, who subsequently became Archdruid of Wales, taking the Bardic title of Trefin. He instilled in me a great love of Wales, which is something that has never left me. My great regret in life is that, living as we did in an anglicised part of Wales, I was insufficiently motivated to learn Welsh.

I never really settled in my new school but I did get up to some wicked pranks there. One day, along with my friend, Keith Pascoe, who lived nearby, I decided to play truant. We walked up the Dram Road, specially constructed for coal wagons, towards the school, hid our school bags in the hedge, and proceeded to the snooker hall in Blackwood Miners' Institute. When we returned to pick up our bags we were petrified to find that they had disappeared. The next step was to go the Police Station. The Sergeant behind the desk had our bags and, to our intense relief, he handed them over without hesitation. His only remark was 'Deuce Alive!' which I remember to this day. My mischievous exploits were some-times found out by my Aunt Elizabeth, who occasionally with a towel in hand, would lash out at me shouting 'YOU FLAMER, YOU FLAMER!' I had a similar punishment after I failed to turn up for my weekly music lesson.

I left school before I was fifteen and spent a few months in a local colliery office but was soon bored with the repetitive nature of the work. Some local boys worked underground in Nine Mile Point Colliery, which was originally called the Coronation Colliery to mark the coronation of Edward VII. It was always known as Nine Mile Point because it marked the halfway stage between Newport and Tredegar. Locally, it was 'The Point' and it was here that my maternal grandfather was a 'sinker', one of the original workers who sank the pit. My paternal grandfather, my father and my mother's brothers all worked there. My father left the pit suffering from the miners' eye disease nystagmus and, as far as I know, he did not receive any compensation. I was told he was a very good collier and at the age of seventeen he had 'a place of his own on the coal', which meant that he was responsible for a length of coal face, work normally undertaken by an adult. This must have been almost unique. His sister, my Aunt Elizabeth, said of him, 'Our John never had an idle bone in his body.'

Nine Mile Point had a record of militancy and I was particularly fascinated by the 'Stay In' strike of October, 1935. This was a demonstration to drive out the 'Scab' union, or the South Wales Miners' Industrial Union to give it its official

title. Workmen had lived locally but the Company drafted in
workmen from twenty miles away by special train to try to
undermine members of the South Wales Miners' Federation.
In protest the 'Stay In' strike started in the West Pit and miners
there were soon joined by men from the East Pit and the Rock
Vein. This form of action spread to other areas of the coalfield
in South Wales. Men in the West Pit stayed underground for
177 hours and in the other two pits for 101 hours. According
to the *South Wales Argus* of 19 October 1935, news spread like
wildfire that the men were to leave the pit.

'Hundreds of people clambered over the colliery fences and
rushed and ran to the colliery premises. Men, women and
children thronged roadways and there was wild cheering when
the first miner appeared.'

The issue of 'Unionism' was not immediately resolved and
it took several more years before the South Wales Miners'
Federation finally achieved one hundred per cent membership
and exclusive negotiating rights in regard to pay and
conditions. Nine Mile Point had become part of the Ocean
Coal Company, which was the creation of (Lord) David
Davies, Llandinam, and today he is regarded as being the
outstanding entrepreneur produced by Wales. At the time of
the 'Stay In' strike the Vicar of Risca, the Revd John Evans, had
written to Lord Davies about the serious dispute at Nine Mile
Point Colliery and all the social hardship that was being caused.
According to the *South Wales Argus* (19 October 1935) 'Lord
Davies expressed his regret about the dispute but that he had
been indisposed for some time and was now leaving on a
recuperative voyage to South Africa.'

Nine Mile Point Colliery was composed of three pits, West
and East, both of which produced steam coal, and the third, the
Rock Vein, which produced house coal. At the age of fifteen I
started to work underground in the Rock Vein and was taught
to drive what was known as a pair of eights. This was a steam

driven fixture with a steel rope and two drums, which pulled the drams of coal out towards the main heading. They were then linked up with drams of coal (known as a journey) from other districts and taken to the bottom of the pit. My classification was that of an engine boy and I was paid twenty seven shillings per week before deduction. The Harris district where we worked involved a one and a half mile walk in each direction. My friend Jack Suter, who lived on Mynyddislwyn mountain where his parents rented a small farm, worked in the Davages district of the East Pit. He had to walk three and a half miles each way to the coal face where he worked. There was no underground transport for workmen in those days.

Winding time for the day shift was between 6.30 and 7.00 a.m. and mid-morning the conveyor belt would be stopped and the overman Jack Edwards would shout, 'Grub Up'. This was our morning break and the food usually consisted of cheese sandwiches and a drink of water from a 'jack' (a tin utensil). The break was only for twenty minutes and then the conveyor would restart. It was a six-day working week at that time but on a Saturday morning we started and finished an hour earlier in order that the boys could get up the pit early to play football. This meant that I had to catch a bus from Pontllanfraith at 4.55 a.m., which was a little early, to say the least. I paid my 'Fed' (Union dues) on a Friday at the end of the shift in a little hut on the opposite side of the road from the colliery premises. At that time there was no deduction at source, which is the usual procedure today.

One or two sad incidents are etched in my memory. A man was killed on the night shift and I recall seeing him being carried across the top of the pit on a stretcher covered by a blanket. Soon, as the men began to come in for the day shift, there was much consternation because there was a tradition that when a person was killed in the pit there was no further work that day as a mark of respect. The colliery manager,

Albert Morgan, (known as Alby) had a somewhat tyrannical image. He rather angrily remonstrated with the Union representatives for the men to work a normal shift because it was war-time and there was a desperate need for coal. The request was, however, refused and we all went home. There was also a tragic incident when a respected minor official threw himself down the pit shaft. When the Police went to his home fairly close to the colliery, they found that he had earlier butchered his wife and daughter.

The Under-Manager in the Rock Vein was a young mining engineer from the Rhondda by the name of Jack Fox. He was rather a rough diamond but I must say he was always very kind to me. In the pithead baths each workman had two lockers, one for his clean clothes and the other for clothing he wore down the pit. The rows of lockers were called Barries and, as it happened, Mr Fox had a locker very close to mine. Nearby also was that of Mr Idris Jones, who, besides working in the pit, kept the Mason's Arms in Blackwood. In those days food was not served in pubs, for they were merely beer houses, and it was quite common for a landlord to have a second job. Idris Jones, I should point out, was the grandfather of the ill-fated former Member of Parliament for Tatton, Neil Hamilton. Mr Fox proceeded to become Manager of Wyllie and Oakdale Collieries and subsequently Group Agent. After I was elected to the House of Commons I asked my close relative, Ifor Gravenor, who was an official on the surface at Oakdale Colliery, if he could get me a miner's lamp as a souvenir. He approached Mr Fox who said, 'Roy and I used to work together. Go to the lamp room and tell them I want two lamps because I will be retiring shortly.' Needless to say that miner's lamp is now one of my most treasured possessions.

During those early war years in Nine Mile Point I began to take an interest in the Young People's Guild in the Church and subsequently became Secretary. We organised debates and other similar activities. We took a decision to form a football team which became known as St Augustine's Young People's Guild. Here, again, I became Secretary and I must have been a real power-seeker in those days. These activities kept my mind active and were an escape route from the pit.

These, though, were the early days of the war and almost everything was either in short supply or unobtainable, so to form a football team in those circumstances was well nigh impossible. Our youthful enthusiasm, however, overcame these difficulties. We were able to obtain some old football jerseys from a team which until the outbreak of war had operated from the Penllwyn, which some of us did not think of as being part of Pontllanfraith at all. Soon we were participating in the Abertillery and District League and eventually won the Cup. In retrospect it is noticeable that the colleagues who were active with me at this time all did well later in life.

My friend Bertie Cripps became the Accountant for Rhymney Urban District Council; Harry Lewis became Clerk of Abertillery UDC; Morris Cole became Head of Eveswell School in Newport; Billy Matthews became Under-Manager in Britannia Colliery and one of our star players, my close friend Derek Jones, subsequently became an Area Manager for British Insulated Calendar Cables and we have remained friends to this day.

At the age of seventeen I was on the Executive of two Football Leagues. Soon the elderly gentlemen who ran Monmouthshire football before the war began to sit up and take notice. They soon got out of the cupboard the silver cups which had been stowed away for the duration of the war. After being polished up, they were put up for competition and, noticeably, the matches were played on Pontllanfraith Miners' Welfare Ground. There was tremendous interest in local football during those war years, for the English leagues had ceased to function and it was before the TV era. It created interest and helped sustain morale during those dark days of the war.

Dancing in those years was very much part of South Wales valley culture and in Blackwood we had a magnificent dance hall at the Miners' Institute. There were other venues nearby such as the Memorial Hall, in Newbridge, which was very popular, but the 'Stute' in Blackwood was a little up-market and young people flocked there from the surrounding district. I had started going dancing when I was about sixteen and I always found it most enjoyable. Together with my friends we enjoyed the big bands and, above all of course, it was an opportunity to meet girls. At the height of the war there was quite a clampdown on leisure activities such as dancing. A gentleman by the name of Mr Sam Nash presided over the Magistrates' Bench until he was past eighty years of age. He was eventually succeeded by Mr Sam Garland, who proved to be equally tough. Dances had to finish by 9.30 p.m. and so-called 'long' dances, held by various organisations and charities, which normally went on until midnight, were cut out altogether. Young girls were recruited into the local munitions factories and when on the night shift they had to leave the dance very early. They changed into what were then known as 'slacks', which they tended to despise as being masculine. Things are so different today!

For us youngsters the early years of the war were exciting times. My friend Derek Jones had moved to Pontllanfraith from the Caerphilly area when his parents became Steward and Stewardess of the local Club. A few years later they moved again and took over another Club in Cefn Fforest which was three or four miles away. Derek made new friends and I joined up with them. There was Bill Dunstan, whose parents had a road haulage company; John (W.J.) Davies, who subsequently became a Captain in the Army; Gwilym Cookshaw, whose parents had come down from Ripon in

Yorkshire earlier in the century, and Ray Lane who was rather a wicked lad, full of fun.

Another lad called Louis Bassini was in our group for a short time. He was a pleasant likeable boy, the son of Italian immigrants who at the time owned a café in Cefn Fforest. Our leisure activities tended to be centred on the weekend when of course cafés were busy. Louis's parents soon insisted that he concentrated on the business so we lost his company. There was rather an interesting sequel after the war when Louis went on a holiday to Italy. It would seem that the Italian police tried to hold him for conscription into the armed forces. He managed to escape across the border and I imagine he was reluctant to visit Italy for the foreseeable future. He subsequently started up his own business in Ebbw Vale and I recall meeting him when he was a supporter of the local rugby club.

A feature of South Wales were the Italian cafés which were everywhere, situated in the High Street and shopping centres of our towns and villages. The immigrants were said to have all come over from the same area of Bardi in Northern Italy around the second half of the nineteenth century when the South Wales coalfield was rapidly developing.

Blackwood, the town a mile from my home, had a host of these cafes and even today the names of their proprietors still come to mind – Restaghini, Minoli, Servini, Carpanini. These establishments were very popular with young teenagers, particularly on a Sunday evening when there was what was popularly known as a 'monkey parade' up and down the main street. Hot snacks, pies, beans on toast and similar snacks could be purchased, together with ice cream delicacies such as North Pole and banana split. No alcohol was sold but a drink called sarsaparilla was very popular with youngsters. It was the equivalent of coke today and the same colour.

There were some difficulties when Italy under Mussolini entered the war on the side of Nazi Germany. Patriotic feelings were running high and I recall the windows of the Square Café in Blackwood being smashed. The proprietors were the Carpanini family who were popular and well integrated into the community. It has since been said that some of these Italian immigrants were being pressurised into contributing funds for the pre-war build-up and the Fascist cause. As for the Square Café, its windows were soon restored and splashed on them in large letters were the words 'Proprietor Tom Thomas', a local businessman whom I came to know well in later years. What sort of business deal was arranged over the acquisition of the premises is a matter of speculation.

On a Saturday evening, unless we went further afield, we had a few drinks (sometimes more) in the Tredegar Arms in Blackwood, which I believe had earlier been called The Old Mill. When we think of the modern sophisticated drinking establishments of today it is worth recalling the facilities then offered by the Tredegar Arms. Our little gang went into a very small room at the back of the pub. The wooden bench-like seating would have been slightly less than a foot wide. Heating was provided from a grate which had been stacked up with duff (coal dust) and there was no trace of any fire. Late in the evening the landlord Mr Edwards, a rather canny character, came in with a poker and gave the so-called fire a stoke up. I recall him vividly. He always wore a cap and tended to mutter to himself. After a few drinks it was 'up the dance' to meet the girls. We always met there because young girls did not drink in those days. Our little gang was broken up somewhat when a number of us were called up to the Forces. We resumed, though, after the war and our numbers increased when Walter Bowen, Vincent Craig, Caradoc Owens, Howell Samuels, Eric Hinds and later John Phillips joined. John was a kind, colourful and argumentative character. He was Manager of the local office of the Department of Social Security. Mrs Bowen, Walter's mother, gave us the name 'The Boys' and this stuck.

Bill Dunstan, Walter Bowen and myself.

We remained great friends for fifty years but now so many of them have passed on.

The group naturally became more mature with the passing years. A tradition was established for us to meet every Thursday evening at the local hostelry. We argued and heatedly debated issues of the day, the fortunes of the Welsh rugby team, with occasional deviations to sex, all from a thoroughly heterosexual viewpoint, I must say. Sometimes people in a pub would sit enthralled listening to our discussions, which were conducted in a most robust manner, although we all remained the best of friends.

Throughout my life I have been plagued with eczema and this was exacerbated by working underground. Eventually I received a doctor's note which enabled me to be released from the colliery. This was something not easily secured during the war when mining was a reserved occupation.

CHAPTER 2

Private R.J. Hughes, 14768574

I WAS CONSCRIPTED into the army early in 1944, Private R.J.
Hughes, 14768574. Several months of rigorous training
(mostly square bashing and field training) followed in Brecon
and Crickhowell. In nearby Sennybridge I was a marksman on
the rifle range. In the Dan-y-parc camp at Crickhowell we
were more than two miles from a bus stop. There were
virtually no cars on the road on account of fuel restrictions.

One day, along with my mate Charlie Tovey from
Blaenavon, I tried to get a lift to Gilwern, a few miles away.
A pickup type of vehicle stopped for us and we jumped into
the back. It was full of large drums of pig swill which spilled
over the top as we slowed down or went round a corner.
Despite the discomfort we arrived in Gilwern and it was a
good laugh.

There were several thousand troops stationed in various
camps in Crickhowell at the time and they tended to drift into
Abergavenny for recreational purposes. One day I said to two
of my mates who came from the Blackwood area, 'Let's go up
to Brynmawr' and so we did. We went to the dance at the
Legion Hall in Nantyglo, which was just down the road. We
had got away from the mob, so to speak, and I may say there
were some very pretty girls in Nantyglo and Blaina.

At the end of this time we were all ready for posting
overseas. There was a rule operating then that the under
nineteens were sent to Europe, for the invasion of the
continent had just got under way. A close colleague from
Blackwood (Ron Jones) was killed almost as soon as he arrived

in France. I was over nineteen and so, with others of this age group, we were taken to Liverpool on a bitterly cold day in December 1944. None of us knew where we were going but when we landed at the docks the dockers quipped, 'It's warmer where you are going.'

A former luxury cruise liner, the *Alcantara*, was the means of transport but as a troopship conditions on it were pretty awful. Our ship was part of a convoy which sailed down the Bay of Biscay, through the Mediterranean (for by then the Allies had recaptured the North African coastline) and through the Suez Canal to Aden and the Red Sea. In the early part of the journey, Charles Tovey, with whom I kept in touch until he died in May 2001, was seriously ill with sea sickness and a stomach infection. I was more fortunate because I contracted a skin complaint (impetigo) and was promptly sent to the Medical Centre on the ship for about a week for fear of contagion. Food and conditions were much better there. While there I met a Scottish lad whose name I cannot remember. The amusing thing was that he could not understand my South Wales valleys accent and I certainly could not understand his Glaswegian. Despite this handicap we got on reasonably well together.

After three or four weeks we saw an unusual looking coastline emerging and soon we were landing in Bombay. The next move was to a transit camp called Kalyan which involved a train journey of some forty miles. Soon I was on the move to the Central Provinces (Budni) for jungle training. In those days the area was part of India of the Princes. One day I remember seeing the Nawab, who was a big fat man in military uniform. He was, I was told at the time, President of the Chamber of Princes. In the Central provinces we had some scary experiences and saw at different times various animals. Once we came across a huge queen cobra which an officer shot with his revolver. Another time at night there was quite a panic when a tiger was spotted near a railway line. These were quite some experiences for young lads who previously had been no further than Cardiff.

The next posting was to Comilla which was essentially a transit camp in North East India, prior to flying into Burma. Some of my colleagues had their hair completely shaved, for they believed it to be more hygienic, but I thought too much of my locks to undergo such drastic treatment. We flew into Burma in a Dakota with the most rudimentary facilities and I recall air pockets when one's stomach almost turned over. Our destination was an airstrip just outside Mandalay on the day that legendary city was recaptured from the Japanese by the 19th Dagger division. Here on 19 December we joined the 2nd Battalion, the Welsh Regiment to which I still have a sentimental attachment because the CO was Lieut. Col. 'Bun' Cowey, the former Newport and Wales three quarter. Travelling around in his jeep was Major General 'Dai' Rees, who of course in later years became Chairman of the Cwmbran Development Corporation. Some years ago I recall being at a dinner in the House of Commons and sitting next to (Peter) Rees, the then Member for Dover who is now in the Lords. We talked about his father and about those days in faraway places.

Soon we were into action and pursuing the Japanese who, although in retreat, were far from defeated. After a day or so a small number of us went out on a patrol. It was a sort of probing exercise to try and find where the enemy was located. There were about ten of us spread out horizontally, each of us carrying a rifle. We made no contact with the enemy but on our return we found that the Japs had shelled our base camp and a colleague, by the name of Samuels from Swansea, was killed. The situation was made more harrowing because his young wife back home was expecting their first child. Until then my attitude had been somewhat casual but at last I realised that this was for real.

Some of the troops had been there for a considerable time and physically were in a poor shape. I recall huge sores on their arms and legs which were a legacy of their long and perilous service in the Burma jungle. Another memory is of seeing so many dead Japanese. Firstly one was faced with a nasty stench and then there was a dead body which had turned black, presumably as a result of the heat. I recall at one stage being based near a tributary of the Irrawadi River, in which we washed. We also drank the water from the river after putting two tablets in our water bottles. The first one was to kill the germs and the second was to restore some sort of drinkable taste. One day as a group of us were washing in the river, something was spotted floating down and when it reached us we realised it was a dead Japanese.

Shortage of water was always a terrible problem and at times our tongues were like cardboard. One day our platoon was out on patrol and as we approached a village we spotted a well. We darted towards it because we were so thirsty but in the event we were severely reprimanded because the well could have been booby trapped and we might well have been blown up.

We were then moved to a hill station and a town called Maymyo. Years later when I was living in Chepstow a family who moved in next door called their house Maymyo. I said to my wife at the time, 'I am sure that is the name of the place where I was based in Burma.' When I checked with my neighbour he confirmed that he had also been stationed there. Their house was called Maymyo because of a pen friendship, which had subsequently blossomed into marriage.

Soon came the news that the war in Europe was over and our forces in South East Asia greeted the news with cynicism. The Forces newspaper out there was called SEAC and was edited by Frank Owen, a close colleague of Michael Foot, who had replaced him as Editor of the *Evening Standard*. It had a cartoon at the time showing about half a dozen troops wearing

Roy Hughes.

their bush hats in the boiling sun and the Sergeant saying to them, 'Break off for ten minutes' smoke – the war in Europe is over.' Weeks later we were on the Toungoo/Mawchi Road with thick teak jungle on either side. The Japanese fought a determined rearguard action and troops were only able to advance about a mile a day. Eventually I was taken out through sickness and sent to Shillong, a hill station in Assam. It was there that I made two new friends, the first called Catt who, prior to his service in the Forces, had been a Civil Servant. The second was called Clarke and he had been a Company representative. Interestingly enough his father was an official of the Transport & General Workers' Union in London. They were both older than me and far more sophisticated. They were keen Labour supporters and because of my interest in politics we became friends. This alliance tended to give me a bit of added confidence. It was at this time that the General Election was being held in Britain but, as I was under twenty-one, I was too young to vote and support the return of a Labour Government with such an overwhelming majority.

Later I was posted to a new unit then based in the South of India but which was about to move up north to Bihar to perform internal security duties. This consisted of moving a small number of troops from place to place to give the impression of a large force when actually there was only a minimal presence.

By now I was following Indian politics very closely and it was the time when the Indian freedom movement was under way. I recall seeing 'Jai Hind' ('Quit India') written on trains, and noisy political meetings were being held in various towns and villages.

At this stage I had my first attack of malaria. The night before leaving on the long train journey to Bihar I was feeling a bit under the weather, so I took the precaution of calling in at the Medical Room. My temperature then was quite normal but the following day it simply soared and I had to be taken off the train and sent to a Forces hospital in Secunderabad in Hyderabad state. Some weeks later I had a further bout of malaria and two further attacks when I returned to Britain. The first was pretty severe but I got over it. In my home village of Pontllanfraith there was a lad from London called Bert Slocombe, but he was always known as 'Snowy White' because of the colour of his hair. He had married a local girl but during the war he had served in the Merchant Navy and was in the Medical Room. He gave me a large bottle of mepacrine tablets and over a period of weeks and months I took the lot. It did the trick and I have never suffered from malaria since.

By now I was much engaged in political discussion and it was considered at the time that the Forces had played a major part in the Labour victory. Politically for me it was an exciting time for in the 1945 General Election a Labour Government had been returned with a large majority. It was not long before the two atom bombs were dropped on the Japanese cities of Hiroshima and Nagasaki. I could not at that time realise the immensity of what had happened but we were all overjoyed because it brought about the end of the Second World War – VJ Day as it became known. Some years ago I had the privilege of visiting Hiroshima with a Parliamentary delegation and I was able to sign the book of remembrance there.

After the war ended we 'festered' for some months but things became very boring and I wrote to my Member of Parliament, Sir Charles Edwards, to obtain early release to return to industry. In due course he sent me the Ministerial reply authorising my release. When I returned to Pontllanfraith the Union Jacks were out in Newbridge Road. Soon, though, memories of the war started to fade and there was a great drive on to get industry back to normal. I had returned to the UK by troopship and was demobbed in Ashton under Lyme. There I received my 'demob suit' and also a trilby hat. Perhaps it was fascination with this latter item that led to the loss of my 'bush hat' in the clothing store. This was a source of some regret but it had served me well. After demobilisation I returned to Nine Mile Point colliery without much enthusiasm but I thought it was better to be at home than stuck out in the Far East.

Soon we had nationalisation of the coal mines. I recall sitting on the colliery steps at Nine Mile Point when a plaque was unveiled by the Lodge Chairman, Arthur J. Davies, indicating that the mines now belonged to the people. A five-day week in the pits quickly followed – a major step forward.

My life-long hero Aneurin Bevan, Minister for Health, brought forward the Bill to create the National Health Service which many still feel was the outstanding achievement of the '45 Government. By this time I had joined the local Labour Party. My ardour was dampened a little, however, by the nature of the discussions which seemed to revolve round such matters as rates, house allocation, refuse collection and road repairs, whereas my chief interest was in national politics and the big issues. I withdrew for a time but then resolved to concentrate on Party activities, whatever the frustrations that might be in my way. I was encouraged when I was appointed to attend a weekend school at Tintern in the Wye Valley. This experience left a lasting impression for it gave me a better understanding of how the Party worked and it was an opportunity to meet colleagues from other areas.

Soon I was made Assistant Secretary of the local party whose meetings were held in the Plaza, Pontllanfraith, which was a hall for dancing and snooker and which had been built and owned by the Harris family, close relatives of my paternal grandmother. I also became a delegate to Mynyddislwyn Trades and Labour Council. This was a very useful forum for the local Party and Trade Union branches to get together, but this type of organisation was later wound up by the National Labour

Party, allegedly because of Communist infiltration. I have to say we had no such difficulty locally and there was resentment at the rather high-handed action of the national party.

At the time, the Secretary of the local Party was a Mrs Margaret Morris, a Northerner who had married Bert Morris, an accountant with the local Council. They both proved to be firm friends and they encouraged me in every way. Mrs Morris seemed keen that I should take over as Secretary and this I soon did. The Chairman of the local Party was Alderman Sidney Jones who had retired a little earlier as Miners' Agent. His knowledge of the Labour and Trade Union movement was immense and much of it came from practical experience. A Marxist, he had been a student at the Central Labour College. I regularly visited his home in Woodfieldside, ostensibly to make arrangements for future Party meetings but my stays often lasted for three hours. When I went to leave he would push me back in my chair and Mrs Jones would come in with cups of tea. Our discussions ranged widely over current political issues and particularly over the history of the Labour movement. These sessions were invaluable for me. It gave me some satisfaction later when I was based in Coventry, and Alderman Parfitt, a former official of the Miners' Union in the Rhondda, was heard to say, 'This boy knows his fundamentals.'

I was soon irritating the management at Nine Mile Point and one or two incidents come to mind. A man called Percy Chivers who was on the administrative staff wrote a letter to the *South Wales Argus* complaining about a lack of co-operation from the miners. The following week I replied and made rather a scathing attack on him which did not exactly please the colliery officials. A local lad Roy John said to me 'If I could write a letter like that I would not be down here.' There was another incident when I made the colliery manager, Orion Powell, look a bit silly in front of a group of workmen. The manager later described me as 'quite incorrigible'. This latter word proved a bit of a tongue-twister for the miners and they were rather amused by it.

After the great victory of 1945 and its major achievements in office, the Labour Government was re-elected with only a tiny majority in 1950. This was despite receiving the highest vote ever for any party in a British General Election. There was discussion in the Party, though, particularly as to the speed and degree of future Socialist advance. Aneurin Bevan resigned from the Government in 1951, mainly on account of NHS prescription charges. This grievance was augmented by the proposed level of defence expenditure which he felt was unsustainable. There was little doubt, too, about the rivalry between Aneurin and Hugh Gaitskell, who had by now become Chancellor of the Exchequer. Aneurin by contrast had been moved sideways by Attlee to Minister of Labour. Bevan could not understand why he, a bona fide working class representative, had been passed over for the middle-class Wykehamist, Hugh Todd Naylor Gaitskell, whom he had obliquely referred to as a desiccated calculating machine. I was present in Ebbw Vale in 1951 when he came back to report to his constituency, after resigning from the Labour Government. What a momentous occasion that was! The meeting was held on a Sunday evening in a large cinema with an overflow gathering outside and I recall the revivalist hymns to greet the 'errant' MP before he appeared on stage. He was rapturously received.

The following morning our neighbour Mrs Harrhy 'knocked the wall' with a poker. It was a sort of bush telegraph because we had no phone in those days. When my Aunt went to the garden fence, Mrs Harrhy exclaimed, 'Your Roy is on the front page of the *Western Mail*.' It was a case of fame at last, or at least a bit of reflected glory.

On the same day I returned from the Forces my friend Derek Jones took me to Aberbargoed to meet his friend Walter

Bowen who had been an apprentice draughtsman with the Powell Duffryn Company, which was taken over by the National Coal Board on nationalisation. Walter subsequently became Chairman of Mid Glamorgan County Council. He soon encouraged me to come to rugby and this was a momentous step, for I developed a passion for the game that has endured for over fifty years. I gave up the Secretaryship of the local soccer club, for I found it occupied too much of my time and I wanted to enjoy myself after my experiences in the Far East. Walter was a keen Cardiff supporter but when we attended a Newport v Cardiff match there was never any doubt as to whose side I supported, because Black & Amber was in my blood. Newport had a great pack in those days and their dominance enabled their outside half, little Roy Burnett, to exploit fully his scintillating skills.

Soon it was 1950 and Twickenham. We managed to obtain ten shilling stand tickets and we stayed at the Regents Palace from Friday until Sunday. The cost was a guinea per night bed and breakfast. Wales had a splendid victory with three Newport backs in the three quarter line, i.e. Ken Jones, Malcolm Thomas and Trevor Brewer. From then on I have never missed an England v Wales match at Twickenham. In the first international of the 1951 season Wales hammered England at Swansea and Malcolm Thomas scored a spectacular try, running almost the length of the field. The game also marked the selection of Glyn Davies at outside half, following the retirement of Bill 'The Kick' Cleaver, whose style of play had brought some criticism.

We had won the Triple Crown in 1950 and the newspapers were speculating about another 'Golden Era' of Welsh Rugby. Five of us young lads in the Pontllanfraith/Blackwood area were determined to go to Scotland for the next fixture and to follow this success story. We hired an old funeral car from 'Lanes', Cefn Fforest, which had seen better days. My colleague Bill Dunstan of the local haulage company was to be the driver and a wonderful driver he was. We started out at 9 a.m. on the Monday before the match because we were afraid to miss the kick-off. Our first stop was Blackpool where we stayed the night. Some of us had been to this famous resort during the summer but at the end of January we found a ghost town. The following morning was bitterly cold and the car would not start. I recall helping to push it along the street, not a particularly pleasant experience after searching out the hostelries of Blackpool on the previous evening! A formidable journey lay ahead, for in those days there were no motorways and drivers had to cope with the notorious Shap Fell. We arrived in Edinburgh unscathed, and what a wonderful city, for its buildings simply reek of history and tradition. What was more the people were so welcoming and we quickly found too that 'McEwans' was a far more potent beverage than 'Rhymney', which had nurtured us in the valleys.

Finally it was the day of the match and despite the travel hazards there was a good Welsh contingent in Edinburgh. As the huge crowd surged in, I recall seeing them pushing along cars in the entrance way. John Gwilliam was our captain and he was a man of stature, besides being a devout Christian. The Welsh team was full of illustrious stars including the legendary Lewis Jones who subsequently went north. Bob Evans was one of the flankers and he was sharing a hotel room with John Gwilliam. On the Friday evening Gwilliam got down to pray at the side of the bed but on this occasion his prayers were not answered. A day that began with such optimism was soon reduced to tears. The game was immortalised by a drop goal, virtually from the touch line, by the Scottish forward Kininmonth. For Wales, nothing would go right and although John Gwilliam switched his team, bringing Lewis Jones in at outside half, it was all to no avail. When the final whistle blew, 19-0 seemed to represent a fair result. Still, Wales soon recovered and in the following 1952 season I was in Dublin to see us win the Triple Crown after one or two spectacular tries by Ken Jones. The rugby international trips were high-spirited adventures with a lot of ale drunk in the process.

Local Authorities at this time were anxious to celebrate the coronation of Queen Elizabeth II and Mynyddslwyn Urban District Council called a meeting of relevant organisations such as the Churches, local industry, the British Legion, Trades Unions and political parties, with a view to establishing a representative committee. As regards political parties, this meant in effect the Labour Party because for practical purposes it was the only political party in the area. I was sent along to represent the Labour Party and, yes, I came out as Secretary, with the vicar, the Revd Leslie Jones, as Chairman. The Committee was formed and a week of celebrations was sug- gested, the only snag being that we had no money. Immediate efforts had to be turned to fund raising. Several hundred pounds was soon raised and this was a lot of money in those days. The celebrations were planned and the whole exercise proved to be a huge success, with many mutual congratulations at the end. On the Committee was a Mrs Gwyneth Pomeroy who I believe represented the National Union of Teachers. I had known her from school days as Gwyneth Richards but she subsequently married Granville Pomeroy who was History Master at Newbridge Grammar School. Later he became Headmaster of Caerleon Comprehensive School.

For some years I had been taking *Tribune* which was closely associated with Aneurin Bevan. In it I had seen advertisements for Coleg Harlech, the adult education establishment which had been the brain child of Thomas Jones of Rhymney, a former Cabinet Secretary. I was half interested in applying for entry but when I mentioned it to Granville Pomeroy he said, 'Why not go for Ruskin?' He encouraged and assisted me in any way he could. I applied for Ruskin and after submitting some written work and attending for interview in London, I was accepted for a two-year Diploma course in Economics and Politics. The only difficulty was that I had no financial backing but this was remedied when I was awarded an adult scholarship by Monmouthshire Education Committee.

I had left the pit several years earlier and was now employed in the office of the Abertillery & District Water Board in nearby Crumlin. They were very good employers and I enjoyed my stay there. For me going to Oxford was very much a journey into the unknown but I quickly made friends with a number of other students. Ron Hughes, a miner from Durham, became a close colleague. The Vice Principal Henry Smith soon advised us, 'Don't let your studying interfere with your education'. This was very wise advice because most of us had come from very limited working-class backgrounds.

It was Michaelmas term and, having joined the Oxford Union, I attended the first meeting of the new term. I was seated among the students when up through the centre aisle strode the new President, Michael Heseltine, in his tails and with those long blond locks. It was all most impressive. At the time the University Labour Club seemed to be flourishing and I joined that too. Anthony Howard, the now well-known writer and broadcaster, was the Chairman and he soon invited Aneurin Bevan to address the members. There was a deep split in the Labour Party and Bevan's coming to Oxford created a good deal of interest. I turned up early and was fortunate to obtain a front seat. Who should come and sit next to me but Michael Heseltine. His seat, however, seemed to have been reserved because of course he was President of the Union. Aneurin, in his speech, said he was rather disgusted with Oxford and presumably he was referring to the lack of support he was receiving there for the rather left-wing causes he was advocating. The students, it would appear, tended to support Gaitskell who was one of their own, so to speak.

At the Rookery in Headington, which was part of Ruskin College and used primarily for student accommodation, there were tennis courts and a snooker table. I could play a useful game of tennis at the time and for this I was considered rather bourgeois. To this kind of comment I retorted, 'Do you know where I learned to play? Penny half an hour on the Miners' Welfare.' I could also play snooker well which was, I suppose, the result of a rather dissipated youth.

As a student I found that marginal utility and the law of diminishing returns were very different from anything I had tackled previously but I managed to cope with the new disciplines. Ruskin College is in Walton Street and adjoining it is Worcester College. At the same time I was in Ruskin there was a bright young undergraduate in Worcester called Peter Fry, subsequently Sir Peter Fry, MP for Wellingborough 1968-1997. I came to know him very well in later years. In Oxford there were all manner of activities going on and we had the opportunity of going to two or three different functions and meetings each evening. Occasionally on a Saturday morning we would go to St John's College to hear a lecture by Professor G.D.H. Cole. One evening I went to a Racial Union meeting, accompanied by a fellow Ruskin student who came from Iran. He was popularly known as Sultan. It was he who introduced me to Marion. She wore a camel hair coat, which suited her blond hair. I was very impressed. That evening I walked her home and all I can say is that we have been together ever since. I discovered Marion worked at Rewley House, the Delegacy for Extra Mural Studies in the University. She was also Secretary of the Cowley & Iffley Ward Labour Party. An outdoor type and a keen rambler, she has a love of literature, art and music, apart from being a devotee of 'Coronation Street'. Marion has been the love of my life, or, as she would put it, 'apart from Rugby and Politics'.

We have three daughters. Rosemary was educated at Kings

College, London, and Hughes Hall, Cambridge. She is now Deputy Head of a Comprehensive School in Glamorgan. Pamela and Meriel took their Master of Arts degrees at Surrey University, Guildford. They both teach German and French. Pamela is also a talented oboist.

It was in 1956 that Marion and I met and the following year we were married at St Luke's Church, Scarborough, which was her home town. There was a bit of Welsh flavour at the ceremony as the Vicar was a native of Pontypridd. We spent our honeymoon in the West of Ireland and we have had a love of that area ever since.

Although not a Catholic, Marion, after winning a scholarship, was educated at Our Lady's Convent, Scarborough, which was part of the Order of the Ladies of Mary, a teaching order. Years later when I was in the House of Commons I remember having a chat in the Tea Room with Lewis Carter-Jones (MP Eccles). The Easter recess was approaching at the time and I asked him if he was going away. He said that he and his wife were going up to the NUT Conference in Scarborough, Pat's home town. 'That's strange,' I said, 'it's my wife's home town, too.' We exchanged our wives' maiden names and it turned out that they had been at the Convent School at the same time, indeed in the same class.

Marion recalls – 'One day at school our English teacher was going through our homework essays one by one. She was so disgusted with our work she (more or less) threw our books at us but when she came to Pat's essay she read it out aloud to us with the comment, "Dickens himself would not disown that."

'In those war-time years there was much dispersal among young people after leaving school. Pat and I went our different ways and lost touch with each other.'

As an eighteen-year-old Wren, Marion was posted to Gayhurst Manor, North Buckinghamshire, which was one of

Marion.

several old houses in the area requisitioned by the Admiralty at the time. All were centred on Bletchley Park, or BP as it was known, the headquarters of British intelligence. Many thousands of servicemen of all branches were engaged in the work, together with civilians with diverse skills and talents, particularly in mathematics and linguistics. Academics and scholars from Universities were also brought in, especially from Cambridge. They were distinguished in their own disciplines and in addition most of them were expert chess players. These diverse people had one thing in common, a total commitment to their work and to silence. The whole operation was central to the war effort and was one of the best kept secrets. It consisted of breaking the German code, the Enigma. They worked round the clock, month after month, through the momentous D-Day landings and until the war effort reached its climax.

Marion recalls – 'Gayhurst was a beautiful Elizabethan Manor with extensive grounds. It had connections with the Gunpowder Plot and indeed there was a narrow lane called Digby's Walk which led from the grounds to the River Ouse. Close to the manor house was a church designed by Sir Christopher Wren. In this connection I am reminded of the GI who was being shown around London. Pointing to St Paul's Cathedral, the guide said, "And there you have a fine example of Wren's work."

"Aw gee" said the GI, "those Wrens sure are a swell bunch of dames."

'The operations were carried out in two large huts, A and B, in a little coppice at the back of the Manor House. Here and at the other outstations the Wrens operated machines called bombes which were identified by the names of pioneers in the electrical field such as Volta, Faraday, Joule, Ampere. There were many different types of bombe, each more sophisticated than the last, but basically they all housed revolving coloured drums at the front of the machine, while at the back was a complicated array of plugs which had to be fitted according to a given plan called a menu. It was said that five miles of wiring went into the simplest of the machines. When the bombe was set in motion, the drums revolved at different speeds; now and again the machine would come to a stop to reveal a scrap of information. I seem to recall it consisted of three numbers and four letters. This combination might be the clue that was being sought. It was then put through some tests on another machine and, if it met given criteria, it was immediately phoned through to Bletchley Park. If it was indeed the sought-after clue, there was a great shout from the tiny office –"Job up on Joule!" The bombes were then stripped and a new menu was immediately forthcoming. The different types of bombe must have reached the limits of intellectual capability at the time and it was estimated by one of the senior staff that the number of permutations it could produce was not far short of 6,000 million million million. Churchill leaned heavily on the Bletchley Park source of intelligence. He once said "They are the geese that lay the golden egg, but they don't cackle."

'The Senior staff at the Park were also faced with the problem of how to keep from the Germans the knowledge that their cyphers were being broken and the revealing of German plans sometimes made it necessary for subterfuges to be brought into play to mislead the enemy. A real Tom and Jerry scenario! One thing I remember vividly is that we knew nothing of the processes which had gone on before our machines were called in, nor anything beyond the completion of our work. This was to be expected and the whole organisation was fragmented in such a way that no one, except a few at the highest level, held more than a tiny piece of the completed puzzle. When in May 1945 the European War came to an end the work collapsed like a house of cards and the disciplines were replaced by high spirits of the custard pie variety.'

CHAPTER 3

'Bliss was it in that dawn to be alive,
But to be young was very heaven.'

IN 1957 I WENT TO Coventry and the night before I left there was an incident which left a lasting impression on me. My Aunt Hilda, who was then living in nearby Ynysddu, came to our house in Pontllanfraith and she beckoned me to go into the front room. There she put in my hand a great wad of notes and I was a bit overcome at such generosity. I could not take the money in such a way. Hilda had what we could call in Wales 'Cardi'* instincts; in other words she could handle money, but both she and my Aunt Elizabeth had a sense of responsibility towards me which was manifested from time to time.

I quickly obtained employment in the office of the Standard Motor Company at the Banner Lane Works, which produced Ferguson tractors. The staff at the Employment Exchange in Cheylesmore half apologised for not being able to offer me something better at the time. What a contrast this was to South Wales, where employment opportunities were so limited. I was interviewed in the back office which I later discovered was only occupied by Managers and Executives. When I went out to the general office it was a huge office/factory and I was somewhat nonplussed. This was the Supplies Department and I was a records clerk. It consisted mostly of mathematical work which I picked up very quickly and in fact in a few months I was teaching the job to other entrants. This went on for six months and then I became further engaged in trade union

---

*Cardigan.

37

work which continued until I was elected to Parliament. At the outset I had joined the Transport & General Workers' Union (Clerical & Supervisory Section) and I remained a card carrying member of that Union for forty years.

I recall during those Banner Lane days the Friday morning jostle when the assembly workers received their pay packets. Some of them would make their way to the outer fencing of the works. Money was then pushed through to their waiting wives. Incidentally, Banner Lane was known locally as Letter Lane as it was in a woodland area.

The late fifties saw sweeping changes in the industry. Mr Alick Dick, Chairman of the Standard Motor Works, sold off the tractor assets to Massey Ferguson and used the proceeds to computerise the Standard industry which now launched the Triumph range of cars. The headquarters was moved to Canley and I was transferred to work there in the Supplies Department. Here a huge computer called Leo was installed and it streamlined considerably the work carried out in this Department. Strangely enough the core of the works was in an old building in Canley called Ivy Cottage. Recently it was demolished, much to the dismay of many people who had memories of it. I was among those who protested.

The Standard Motor Company then had six factories in Coventry employing some 10,000 people. The trade union branch I belonged to had about 800 members. I quickly got elected as the representative for the Supplies Division and at this time I became close friends with a very pleasant lad called Don Hinson. There had been some mismanagement of the finances of the Union Branch and a vacancy arose for Secretary. Don was keen that I should take on the job but I had only been there a short time, so I prevailed on him to stand for election. Unfortunately he was not in office very long owing to some domestic difficulties and Jack Jones, who had just moved to Birmingham as Midlands Regional Secretary of the Union, asked me to take it on. It involved quite a lot of work and I had about twenty collectors in the different factories and departments. At the end of each quarter the books had to be balanced and returns submitted to the Regional Finance Office. Marion and I spent four late nights on this work.

I quickly discovered that our members, staff workers, were not being treated at all fairly. This was largely due to a lack of militancy. By comparison the manual workers had a tightly knit trade union structure and were well paid. The Chairman of our Branch at this time was a good colleague, Edgar Emerson, who had come to Coventry from the Rhondda Valley. We produced a manifesto, pointing to the relatively poor pay of our members but indicating that 'the winds of change' were now blowing through their ranks and a new, more militant spirit was emerging. This caused quite a stir at the time and we were soon backing it up with a wage claim. The management rejected it and this was followed by a mass walk-out. This was the sort of militancy that had not been demonstrated before by staff workers. Next morning the headlines of the *Daily Worker* read 'Red Blooded Action by White Coated Workers'. We went back to the negotiating table and the management conceded a general increase of ten shillings a week. This was the equivalent of about £5 or £6 in today's currency and we all felt reasonably pleased with the outcome. This at least was a step forward. Over the next year or two there were a number of confrontations with the management. On one occasion they got a bit fed up with us and it seems that Jack Jones had been contacted. He in turn asked the Branch Chairman and me to come to Birmingham to meet him. There he told us in the nicest possible way to keep within the rules of procedure. I have always had the highest possible regard for Jack Jones and over the years I came to know him well. His late wife Evelyn was a most charming lady.

There was another dispute in the Accounts Division over

deplorable working conditions and a stoppage took place
when the department was due to provide a Quarterly Report
which was of some urgency and importance. The outcome
was that Jim Mahers, who had taken over as Branch
Chairman, myself and one or two representatives, found
ourselves in the office of Coventry & District Engineering
Employers. There we were faced with the Director, a Mr
Weekes, and representatives of the Company. Mr Weekes
threatened me in particular that if there was a repeat of such
an incident I would be frogmarched out of the factory gates. I
must say that for me such a threat had little effect because I
can truthfully say that no Headmasters, Bosses, or Whips for
that matter, ever really frightened me. We endeavoured to
achieve one hundred per cent trade union membership among
the clerical and supervisory staff throughout all the factories of
the Standard Motor Company. This was not an easy task, for
some imagined themselves a little superior to belong to a
Union and a smile from the bosses would make their day. We
tried to impress on the staff the fact that the manual workers
were getting good wages because they had such a tightly
organised trade union structure.

One fascinating department at the Canley Works was the
'Cashiers'. It was ringed around with a high steel fence, almost
like a zoo. It employed many girls who, for alleged security
reasons, were not allowed to join the Union. The Cashier was
a 'hail fellow well met' character with a handlebar moustache.
Apart from his deputy the remainder of the staff were female.
All wages then were paid in cash and as so much money was
being handled one could understand the need for security. We
tried to get the staff into the Union but the Cashier would
have none of it.

One day a buzz went around the factory that a large sum of
money had gone missing from the department. The Police
were called in and I recall that the Deputy Cashier was

interrogated for quite a long time. Some people speculated that he might be the prime suspect but he was not arrested. Personally I felt very sorry for the poor man because he seemed a straight dealer. The whole matter blew over but then, a year or two later, a similar incident occurred. This time the Police had no hesitation in arresting the Cashier himself. He was charged, put on trial and eventually received a hefty prison sentence. There was a sequel to this chain of events. By now I had become a member of the City Council and served on the Education Committee besides a number of its Sub-committees. I recall sitting on a Subcommittee when the Director of Education, the formidable Mr Chinn, revealed that he had received an appeal for financial support for a young lad in public school whose father had been a finance officer at a local car plant but was now in prison. It soon emerged that the gentleman concerned was the former Cashier at the Standard Motor Company. Needless to say the financial request was turned down and I may say it did not receive any support from me. I have often thought that it was no wonder that he did not wish the Union to recruit his staff. The fewer people who knew about his department the better it was from his point of view.

The Standard Motor Company, or British Leyland as it became known after the takeover in 1960, was a large enterprise employing some ten thousand people. The vast majority of this number were hourly paid and owing to the demand for cars, together with a solid trade union organisation, they were well remunerated. In my position as the senior staff representative covering six factories I often had to go and see different managers when there was a grievance. Once there was a case of a man who had worked some overtime and had not been paid. He was told it would be in his pay packet the following week. I went to see his manager who indicated that he was unable to rectify the situation, but my demand was that the man had worked the hours and now he wanted the money. One word led to another and eventually the manager angrily threw his wallet at me. 'Take it,' he said.

There was a recognised trade union practice that no representative (shop steward) went before a manager alone. To do so might suggest that he was collaborating with management and doing a secret deal. Some managers could be bullies and we had many female members. If any incident occurred which needed investigation I, together with a colleague, would go in and 'flatten the bugger', as we put it. He tended to be more compliant after our visit.

Another tactic we would use with an awkward manager was to ignore him and go above his head to higher management. He would then be sent for to give an account of himself. It was rather humiliating to be asked what was the trouble in his department, the inference being that he was not controlling things harmoniously. Our main endeavour, though, was to inculcate into the members the idea that they had to stand together if they were going to improve their pay and conditions. Senior management would say, 'Of course we would like to deal with our staff as individuals.' A story was circulated of a man who had been called in by his manager and given a ten shilling increase in his wages. There were inferences of 'mum's the word' and he imagined he was the best paid man in the department. To his dismay he later found out that he was the lowest paid.

The management at the Standard appointed a Mr Harris as Head of Security. He had previously been Deputy Chief Constable in the city. When we had a one-day strike over a pay claim he brought in mounted police around the factory gates. There was no trouble, however, apart from the annoyance caused by a handful of blacklegs who slipped in by the back door, so to speak. There were some whom we could never persuade to join the union but yet they were all too ready to accept any benefits forthcoming as a result of collective action. As to this, they were without principles.

For some months after I was elected to Parliament, we still lived in Coventry and one Friday morning I called at the Standard works. I went through the factory gate and proceeded to go into the entrance which I would normally have done when I worked there. All the security staff, about a hundred in number, the police and fire service, were our members and I had a splendid relationship with them. On this occasion, however, a man shouted rather aggressively, 'Round the main entrance.' I thought this was not a very good welcome but I later discovered he had been recruited shortly after I left and was now Head of Security. I went into the main entrance with all its memorabilia and greenery and there stood the Commissionaire in his full regalia. When he saw me his face simply lit up. He recalled of course that he was one of our members whom the management were going to sack. I intervened on his behalf and he was still in a job. This was my farewell to the Standard and I think it is how I would like to be remembered.

In those days Coventry was a fabulous industrial city with huge enterprises employing thousands of people. Large sections of the motor industry were there, together with many component factories: the machine tool industry, aircraft, Rolls Royce, Courtaulds, Dunlop tyres and many more. The revenue in rateable value to the City Council was enormous and with a 'Socialist' Labour-controlled Council these large amounts were spent to rebuild and develop the city for the good of its citizens. It was a situation where it could truly be said 'Nothing is too good for the workers'.* Personally I revelled in it all. It was so different from South Wales, for my

---

*This saying is attributed to Jimmy Thomas, a son of Newport, which I was later to represent in the House of Commons. He became a Member of Parliament for Derby and was subsequently a Cabinet Minister but was forced to resign over a Budget Leak.

granny, so to speak, was no longer living round the corner and I was able to give free rein to my natural aspirations. It was quite a melting pot, for people flocked in from Ireland, Scotland, Wales and the North of England. Some held down two or even three jobs.

In 1958 I came down from Coventry when the Royal National Eisteddfod was held in Ebbw Vale. There is a tradition that on the Sunday evening a *Cymanfu Ganu* (Festival of Song) is held when the English language is allowed. After that it is 'Welsh only' throughout the week. Paul Robeson was the principal guest on this occasion. He had just been allowed out of the United States and had come to South Wales to say thank you, particularly to the South Wales miners who had given him every possible support during his time of conflict with the US Government during the McCarthyite period. The Eisteddfod pavilion is moved each year to wherever the Eisteddfod is being held and it is estimated that it holds some 9,000 people. That evening the singing in Ebbw Vale was sublime. The conductor, who was small in stature, turned to the assembly and said, 'There cannot be better singing in heaven.' Paul Robeson sang a number of his classics, 'Ol' Man River' and so on, besides expressing his gratitude to the people of South Wales. At the time there was an anomalous situation as to whether Monmouthshire was in England or Wales, although the residents did not have any doubt as to where Ebbw Vale was situated. Aneurin Bevan spoke and he looked every inch the statesman. He left no one in doubt about his feelings of Monmouthshire being in Wales and expressed other patriotic sentiments which were received enthusiastically by the audience. It was altogether a memorable evening.

I was also appointed a delegate to the Coventry & District Committee of the Confederation of Shipbuilding & Engineering Unions. This was quite a prestigious body. My knowledge of the engineering industry was infinitesimal but at the end of my first meeting the Secretary, Harry Urwin, said 'Come and have a half-pint.' This was a most welcome gesture. Harry had by this time taken over from Jack Jones as Coventry District Secretary of my Union (T&GU) and he was responsible in the District for 80,000 members. He proved to be a most kind and loyal friend.

Besides my trade union activity I quickly became Secretary of the Coventry North Constituency Labour Party whose Member of Parliament was Maurice Edelman. One Saturday morning Maurice asked me to join him and Richard Crossman for lunch in the Leofric which was a posh hotel in the centre of the city. When the waiter came to take our order Crossman said, 'Let's have minestrone soup, the food of the Italian peasants.' I had never tasted it before and this description has remained with me ever since.

Soon I moved from the Foleshill district to Tile Hill. There I was active in the Coventry South Constituency and became very close friends with the Secretary, Gordon Daly, who was a teacher. I stood for the City Council several times in Tory held seats but then I was elected for the Radford Ward. Councillor Bill Parfitt who came from the Rhondda was made an Alderman and I took his seat. The Leader of the City Council was Alderman Sidney Stringer who had a great deal of experience in local government. His wife Gladwys was from Blaenau Ffestiniog and Welsh speaking. She was a most kind lady and because of my Welsh background I quickly became a favoured son.

We were allowed to serve on four major Committees. Alderman Stringer said, 'I am putting you on a little Committee, 'Estates'. I soon discovered that this 'little' Committee owned the freehold of half the City of Coventry. The following year I was made its Vice-chairman. I also served on the Education Committee which was a major commitment owing to its many and important subcommittees. My third appointment was to the Water & Fire Brigades and the final one was the Watch Committee.

Coventry owned a one third share in the large Clywedog dam in Mid Wales, the other two thirds belonging to the City of Birmingham. The construction of the dam had caused great controversy because it involved the flooding of a village. A delegation which included myself was appointed to visit the dam. The group consisted of Alderman Stringer, Alderman Bill Parfitt, who had by now become Deputy Lord Mayor, the Chairman of the Education Committee, Tom Locksley, who originally came from Pontypool, Alderman Bill Sheridan, with an Irish background, whose wife was from Nantyglo, and Councillor Tom McLatchie. The latter was a Protestant from Glasgow and a keen Rangers supporter. We lunched rather well in Llanrwst. Councillor McLatchie, I recall, was a large Henry VIII type figure, who had a reputation for being something of a gourmet. Towards the end of the meal he asked the young waitress for some Camembert. She replied, 'Sorry, sir, I don't speak Welsh.' We were issued with red safety helmets and proceeded to walk up the incline towards the dam. Then the singing broke out 'We'll keep a welcome . . .' It was all rather hilarious, for most of us were coming back to Wales. It was quite a visit.

My duties on the Watch Committee involved the viewing of possible pornographic films and deciding whether they should be shown in the city. The Police used to come and pick me up on a Sunday morning. One day we were shown a film with an Apache dance and the male dancer pulled out a flick knife and slashed down the middle of his partner's dress – result, total top exposure. When we came to the adjudication, an elderly Conservative, Alderman Harry Weston, said 'Nothing wrong with that. I had my first meal from one of them.'

My close friend Gordon Daly was a Catholic and a pillar

of the Church. He served as an ex-officio member of the Education Committee, representing the National Union of Teachers. His wife, Marie, was Deputy head of a Catholic School, St John Vianney, who, it is said, was the only Catholic priest to become a saint. Gordon persuaded me to become a Governor of this school and it was quite a new experience. At the time the headship was vacant and we eventually appointed a man by the name of O'Leary who originally came from Mountain Ash in Glamorgan. One weekend I travelled back to Pontllanfraith to see my relatives and on the Friday evening I went to the Ifor Arms which was my favourite pub. It was kept by my good friend Mrs Olive Mitchell and her husband Jim, who had been the policeman in the village for nearly thirty years. Sitting at the bar was the Catholic priest who served in Newbridge. I got talking to him and mentioned that I was a Governor of a Catholic School in Coventry. He said, 'What is the name of the School?'

'St John Vianney,' I replied.

'What is the name of the Headmaster?' he asked.

'Mr O'Leary,' I said, 'and he is from Mountain Ash.'

'That is my brother,' was his reply.

I thought to myself, 'What a small world.'

Alderman Parfitt now became Lord Mayor and he endeavoured to give his year of office a lot of Welsh flavour. Cardiff rugby team were playing Coventry at Coundon Road and the Lord Mayor invited both teams to dinner after the match. The dinner was held in the ancient St Mary's Guildhall which the principal guests approached by way of a spiral staircase. David (Dai) Hayward was Captain of Cardiff. He was a valley boy from Newbridge and a flank forward. Rather an aggressive player, he was capped for Wales on a number of occasions. Before the dinner there was a reception and I introduced Dai to the Welsh members of the Council. There was Councillor Mrs Elsie Jones from Crosskeys, Gwent, Harry

Richards from the Rhondda, Tom Locksley, Pontypool, and a number of others with Welsh connections. Dai said to me, 'Tell me, Mr Hughes, where will the dinner actually be held?' and I explained the location to him. Later, we had the call from the MC. 'Make way for the Lord Mayor and his important guests.' When people on the top table took their places, each one had a huge nut and bolt on the plate before him. These had apparently been misappropriated from a builder's yard the previous evening. This was a good start to what turned out to be a gala evening – sometimes bordering on to the riotous.

CHAPTER 4

Towards Westminster

A T THIS TIME Coventry Borough Labour Party embraced
three constituencies. It had a highly successful weekly tote
scheme and plans were afoot to build a new Party
Headquarters. It was discovered, however, that there were
certain discrepancies in the running of the scheme which
undermined the confidence of the punters. New full-time
officials were appointed but a year or two later a decision was
taken to dispense with full-time agents altogether. Then a new
part-time Secretary had to be appointed. I was nominated for
this post and after a ballot at a well-attended meeting in the
AEU hall I was elected. My opponent, Jack Parry, was a local
Probation Officer. This was 1962 and my new post was a
formidable undertaking, particularly as I was already Secretary
of a large trade union branch and a City Councillor. These
commitments involved much hard work and dedication.

I attended the 1962 Conference of the Labour Party. The
principal debate of the week was on the Common Market with
the arguments put forward for and against our membership. I
was anxious to put my point of view, for I had never supported
the idea of Britain joining. Harold Wilson was chairing the
conference that year and people like Lord Shinwell, Frank
Cousins and Bill Carron, President of the AEU, were being
called to speak. Then the Chairman pointed in my direction. I
was wearing a light check sports coat and by my side stood a
very dark burly man who strode up to the rostrum. Then the
Chairman said, 'No, the delegate in the light coat.' The
disappointed delegate was none other than the late Robert

Maxwell. In the next ten years or so I spoke regularly at Annual Conference and often in opposition to Britain belonging to an institutionalised Europe.

Nationally there had been tragedy for the Labour Party. Aneurin Bevan had died from cancer in 1960 and I grieved terribly over his passing. For me there was no one quite like him in politics and he had inspired me as a youngster. There was further difficulty in 1963 when Hugh Gaitskell, the Leader of the Party, died from a mysterious virus. Harold Wilson was subsequently elected leader and I organised his first public meeting. It was a packed meeting held in the Belgrade Theatre in Coventry on a Sunday afternoon.

The General Election was looming and Harold Wilson hit upon the idea of harnessing technology to socialism as a theme for the campaign. To illustrate this theme he came to the new Lanchester College in Coventry. Here, photo shots were taken of him in the laboratory amongst the test tubes, clad in a white jacket and accompanied by his advisor, Dr Tommy Balogh. As Party Secretary I was present on this occasion, as was the Lord Mayor, Alderman Parfitt, the Leader of the Council, Alderman Stringer and Councillor Tom Locksley, Chairman of the Education Committee.

Labour won the 1964 General Election by a narrow margin and we won the Coventry South seat when Bill Wilson defeated Philip Hocking who had won in 1959. For several years I had been on the 'B' list of possible Parliamentary candidates which essentially consisted of nominees of Constituency parties. Then the T&GWU opened its panel and I was nominated for what was known as the 'A' list. Firstly I went to Birmingham for an interview by Jack Jones, the Regional Secretary, and a small committee. The next hurdle was an interview in London with Frank Cousins, General Secretary of the Union, and a subcommittee of the General Executive Council. It was rather interesting that Frank Cousins did not wish me to go into politics and was keen that I should stay with the Union. I replied, nevertheless, that I was essentially a political animal. I wonder what would have happened to me if I had taken up a full-time career in the Union.

Coventry had been razed to the ground as a result of German bombing in the Second World War. It subsequently gained a reputation as something of an international city, particularly through the pioneering of town twinning. The first link had been made with Stalingrad which had also suffered very badly as a result of its heroic battle to halt the German onslaught. Another link was with Kiel in Schleswig-Holstein which had been a major submarine base during the war. Each year a function was held called Kieler Woche and I suppose our nearest equivalent would be the Henley Regatta. A delegation from Coventry City Council was invited to join their festivities and I was included in it, together with Alderman Parfitt and another Councillor. This was a great opportunity and I enjoyed it immensely. Kiel, of course, was the capital of Schleswig Holstein and it gave me my first experience of Regional Government. The Welsh Assembly in Cardiff, though, was very much in the distant future.

A year or two later I was again fortunate to be appointed to visit Czechoslovakia, together with the very senior Alderman, George Hodgkinson. We were twinned with Ostrava, a large industrial city close to the Polish border and also near Lidice, the village that had been destroyed by the Nazis in retaliation for the assassination of Reinhard Heydrich, their local administrative head. While in Ostrava I enquired about the Sudetenland and I was shown a map ringed all round the borders of Czechoslovakia. The Germans living in this area had indicated that they wished to go back to the Fatherland. I was told, 'At the end of the war we granted their wish and packed them all off.'

At this time one of the main issues in Coventry was the building of the new cathedral. There had been some opposition to this plan, particularly from those who argued that resources would be better used to build houses for the homeless. The old cathedral had been almost destroyed by German bombs in the Second World War and was beyond repair. The new building, however, played a significant part in reconciliation with post-war democratic Germany, or the Federal Republic as it became known. The new cathedral was designed by Sir Basil Spence and truly captured the spirit of the age. It was opened by HM the Queen in 1962. Coventry's reputation was as a major industrial centre but now the new cathedral turned it into a tourist attraction as well. People travelled there from all over Britain and from overseas to see this new creation.

In the Radford Ward, which I represented on the Council, were two other Councillors, Wilf Spencer and Bill McKiernan. The former was the more senior member and a Committee Chairman. He was deputed to attend a Local Government Conference at Great Yarmouth and during the course of the week a Mystery Tour was arranged for the delegates. Councillor Spencer went on the trip but to his surprise he landed back in Coventry, for the idea was to visit the new cathedral. Needless to say, he had seen it many times. Being a conscientious Councillor, he planned to take up some matters with his Chief Officer. As he approached the Council House (HQ of the Council), who should be coming along the road but his wife. 'I thought you were in Great Yarmouth,' she remonstrated. Needless to say my fellow Ward Councillor had some explaining to do.

At the time of the October 1964 General Election I was Secretary of Coventry Borough Labour Party. It was my task to organise the meeting which Harold Wilson addressed in the Police Hall. Such was the enthusiasm that there was an overflow meeting outside. People sensed that change was in the air after thirteen years of Tory rule. Emrys Jones, the Regional Secretary of our Party based in Birmingham, came on the telephone and asked me to go down to a jeweller's in the city centre and purchase something of Coventry significance, which the Lady Mayoress would present to Mary Wilson. I found a compact with a Coventry crest on it which had been earmarked for someone who was travelling by ship to America. In the event, the boat had departed before the compact was ready so I was in luck. In the evening, however, Mary Wilson did not appear and it was said that she was not well. The compact was given to Harold so that he could hand it to her. After I was elected to the Commons in 1966, one of the first things Harold Wilson did was to invite the newly elected members to a reception at Number Ten Downing Street. I spoke to Mary Wilson and asked her if she had liked her Coventry gift and she was full of praise and thanks. Mrs Wilson is a lovely lady but I always tended to get the impression that she did not take very easily to public life.

In the General Election of 1964 when he was first elected to power, Harold Wilson expressed the need to modernise Britain. On Saturday 17 October 1964, a new Ministry of Technology was created and the man appointed to run it was the General Secretary of the Transport and General Workers' Union, Frank Cousins. Through being a lay officer of the Union and attending and speaking at its conferences, I had got to know him reasonably well. I had witnessed how confidently he handled a multiplicity of motions at the Biennial Delegate Conference of the Union and its Rules Conference. In my eyes he was a giant of a man and I could well understand why Wilson was keen to have him in the Government. There had been a precedent, of course, when Churchill during the Second World War appointed Ernest Bevin as Minister of Labour, which was hugely important bearing in mind the need

to harness our manpower to the full. Bevin had been the
virtual founder of the TGWU in the early twenties. Though
taunted by the Tories in the House of Commons to expose his
lack of parliamentary experience, he did not allow them to
undermine him in the very important task he had undertaken
in a wartime situation.

Besides having no parliamentary experience, Cousins had
the additional burden of creating a new department from
scratch. He had no Headquarters, no staff, and perhaps more
important still, no funds. There was the additional handicap in
that he did not enter Parliament until January 1965. He was
elected for Nuneaton after Frank Bowles, the sitting Member
for that constituency, was given a seat in the House of Lords.
Soon backbench Tories tried to make Cousins look silly by
exposing his lack of knowledge of parliamentary niceties and
procedures.

In October 1964 Wilson had also created a new Department
of Economic Affairs as a sort of counterbalance to the Treasury.
George Brown was appointed to head it with the rather
grandiose title of First Secretary. He was soon pushing for a
'Prices and Incomes' policy to curb inflation by restricting pay
increases, but Cousins quickly told him it would not work.
There was a so-called 'Declaration of Intent' and, though it was
supported by the TUC, in practice it caused no end of trouble.

In Coventry I had come under the wing of Jack Jones and
Harry Urwin, who were positively opposed to a statutory
incomes policy. This was the viewpoint that I embraced when I
entered the House of Commons. In Cabinet Committees
there were clashes between Brown and Cousins, but Harold
Wilson tried to play down the difficulties, particularly as he
wanted to keep Cousins in the Government. Eventually,
though, in July 1966 Frank Cousins resigned from the
Government to return to his old post as General Secretary of
the TGWU. The Government continued to be plagued by

industrial relations and eventually it led to Barbara Castle and her disastrous document 'In Place of Strife'. It is, I feel, interesting to point out that in his diaries dealing with the latter years of the Wilson Government and its eventual downfall, Crossman seems to express the view that Cousins had been right. He, at least, had the knack of understanding the viewpoint of ordinary people which so many in the Cabinet seemed to lack.

As we were approaching the run-up to the 1966 General Election, I had a phone call from Harry Urwin who by now was the number three in my trade union. 'We are nominating you for Newport,' he said and this was a major development for me. In Gwent, where I was born and brought up, Newport was our town. It had been a Labour seat since 1945 but before that it had been held by Reginald G. Clarry for the Conservatives. He had won a most important by-election in 1922 for the party. It is considered that the name '1922 Committee' was taken from the date of this by-election. This Committee is of Tory back benchers and its Labour equivalent is the Parliamentary Labour Party. Each meet weekly when Parliament is in session. At the time the *South Wales Argus* reported that 'the workers of Lysaghts voted Tory to a man'. This was the huge steel complex on the outskirts of the town which tended to dominate Newport until the end of the Second World War. It was then scaled down and its steelmaking operation was transferred to the new Abbey Works at Port Talbot. As a result of this victory the confidence of the Conservative Party was restored and they felt they no longer needed the backing of Lloyd George. The following day they held a meeting at the Carlton Club at which Stanley Baldwin moved a motion that they break with the coalition. This was carried and the Prime Minister, David Lloyd George, was forced to call a General Election. In the event he never held office again.

First, though, I had to face a selection conference. Fortunately, the Chairman of the Newport & District Committee of the T&GWU was a man called George Thomas, who had heard me speak at the Biennial Delegate Conferences of the Union and had apparently liked what he had heard. Cliff Thomas, the District Secretary of my Union, was from Aberbargoed and he was most helpful. Connie Stevens was an activist in the shop workers' union and when their nominee was not short-listed she did everything she could to support my candidature. She was a formidable lady.

I had two main opponents on the shortlist: firstly, Councillor Aubrey Hames, a local man and a popular figure, and secondly, David Marquand, an academic who I felt was the Transport House★ nominee. His father Professor Hilary Marquand had been a Minister in the Attlee government. Approximately one hundred delegates attended the Selection Conference which was held in the Labour Hall in Stow Hill. I comfortably topped the poll in the first ballot and won an overall majority in the second. Aubrey Hames was the runner up and he subsequently led the Council in Newport for some years. He was always most friendly and helpful to me. There were some suitable celebrations later that evening before I finally reached my old home in Pontllanfraith. My wife had gone up to Scarborough to be with her mother who was seriously ill. She died just before I was elected to Parliament in March 1966. At the time Marion was expecting our third daughter, Meriel.

Harold Wilson announced the date of the General Election as 31 March, so preparations in Newport had to be made quickly. It was a straight fight between Peter Temple Morris (Conservative) and myself. I was a new candidate but together with Party activists I canvassed the constituency and spoke at various meetings. My opponent toured the town pulling a

---

★The then HQ of the Labour Party in London.

My mother and our three daughters on holiday in Cornwall.

yacht behind his car. It bore the slogan 'Blue Peter – not the Red Flag'. The count took place at the Civic Centre and the Mayor, Councillor Alf Lovell, was the presiding officer. He read out the figures: 'Mr R.J. Hughes, 32,098, P. Temple Morris, 21,599', which was a decisive victory for Labour. I was naturally delighted but I realised that great credit was due to those who had worked so hard to bring about such an excellent result. It is interesting to note that Peter Temple Morris, who subsequently represented Leominster for the Conservatives, now sits on the Labour benches in the House of Lords and we are on quite friendly terms.

For the first time since it was created a Parliamentary constituency in 1918 Newport now had a man of Gwent as its representative in the House of Commons. My earlier political activity, though, had of course been in the then Bedwellty constituency, now called Islwyn, which included my old home Pontllanfraith. From 1918 to 1950 it had been represented by

My first election, March 1966.

Sir Charles Edwards who became Labour Chief Whip. On his retirement he was succeeded by Harold Finch, who, although not a miner, nevertheless worked in an administrative capacity for the South Wales Miners in Cardiff where he specialised in compensation matters. When I was first elected to Parliament Harold Finch was just past retiring age. At this time I met County Councillor Maggie Edwards of Wyllie, who said to me, 'Why didn't you wait for us?' Likewise Councillor Bert Mayo of Pontllanfraith said to my brother, 'I thought Roy was coming here.' Had I become MP for Bedwellty it is interesting to speculate what might have happened, for waiting in the wings was a young ginger-haired lad in his middle twenties from Tredegar – Neil Kinnock. Eventually in 1970 he became MP for Bedwellty, defeating the miners' nominee Lance Rogers after a tied ballot in the first round.

My immediate predecessor was Sir Frank Soskice, whom Harold Wilson had made Home Secretary when Labour came to power in 1964. He had rather an unusual background, having been born in Russia. His father had been Secretary to the Kerensky Government, which was the interim administration after the fall of the Czar and before Lenin and the Bolsheviks took over. Harold Wilson is reputed to have said of him 'Frank stands for two things. No more nationalisation and restoration of the Czar.' He was, however, a most kind and friendly man and once I became the candidate he was very helpful. When electioneering had commenced, I was standing at the top of Stow Hill with Sir Frank Soskice. He very proudly said, 'The Chartists marched down here' and my reply was 'Oh yes, I am well aware of that. It was our people who did the marching.' When Sir Frank was made a Life Peer he took the title Lord Stowhill.

Of great importance to the history of Newport was the Chartist rising which took place on a cold wet November night in 1839. It was not at all a sudden uprising in South Wales but was the culmination of a long struggle which had for many years been taking place in different parts of Britain. The object of the Chartist demonstration in Newport was to demand liberation of one of their leaders, who was in prison there.

The Chartists' demands were as follows:-
- that every man of full age should have a vote
- that the property qualification for entry to Parliament should be abolished, which would enable even a poor man to be eligible for election
- that Members of Parliament should be paid
- that voting should be by secret ballot
- that there should be equal electoral districts
- that Parliament should be re-elected every year

These demands, backed by a petition containing 1,250,000 signatures, were rejected in Parliament in June 1837 by 237 votes to 48.

It will be noted that in the People's Charter, as it was called, there was no reference to women's voting rights That was to come nearly a century later. All the demands in the Charter have now been met, with the exception of the annual re-election of Parliament which is hardly feasible and would no doubt lead to instability. Nevertheless, a new session of Parliament is obligatory each year and legislation lapses if it has not been passed by both Chambers. There is no doubt that the Chartists' aims form the basis of our democracy.

Returning to the Newport demonstration, Alexander Cordell has described it vividly.

> The pot that had simmered for fifty years boiled over. Colliers and miners, furnacemen and tram-road labourers were flooding down the valleys to the Chartists' rendezvous; men from Dowlais under the Guests, Cyrarthfa under the Crawshays, Nantyglo under Bailey and a thousand forges and bloomeries in the hills; men of the farming Welsh, the Staffordshire specialists and the labouring Irish were taking to arms.

The Chartists marched from three valleys centred on Blackwood in the Sirhowy Valley, Pontypool in the Eastern Valley and Ebbw Vale in the Western Valley. During the long march to Newport they converged outside the town and marched down Stow Hill to the Westgate Hotel where the troops were garrisoned. They opened fire on the protesters killing twenty-two and injuring many more. One of the dead was a young lad called George Shell who, before he set out, wrote this letter to his parents.

Pontypool, Sunday night

3 November 1839

Dear Parents,
I hope this will find you well, as I am myself at this present. I shall this night be engaged in a glorious struggle for freedom, and should it please God to spare my life I shall see you soon, but if not grieve not for me, I shall have fell in a noble cause. My tools are at Mr Cecil's and likewise my clothes.

Farewell, Yours truly, George Shell.

The carnage was over in twenty-five minutes. Thirty-eight protesters were subsequently arrested and brought to trial in Monmouth. Three ringleaders, Zephaniah Williams, William Jones and John Frost (a former Mayor of Newport) were convicted and sentenced to be hanged, drawn and quartered. Their lives were spared, however, and they were sentenced to transportation for life. The men who lost their lives on this momentous occasion are now honoured by a memorial in the grounds of St Woolos Cathedral in the town.

Now in Newport town centre can be seen an arresting mosaic depicting the uprising. The Westgate Hotel is very much part of Newport's history but in recent years it has lost out to large out-of-town hotels with parking facilities. Now it is being converted into a shopping mall while retaining the elegant facade. I am reminded of Max Boyce's song 'The pithead baths are a supermarket now.' But the bullet holes remain.

Newport was an impressive monument to Victorian architecture for it developed rapidly at the end of the nineteenth century with the expansion of coal exports from the docks. But like so many towns and cities the old fabric suffered badly from redevelopment in the fifties. Throughout Britain at that time it was a case of 'out with the old, in with the new' and we now regret deeply the damage that has been done to our heritage. One of the local historians used to advise us to 'walk high', looking not so much at the plate glass shops at ground level, but above at the remaining Victorian buildings.

When electioneering in Newport I often came across groups of young people who were not exactly interested in the political scene. I would ask them, 'Do you ever go to the Westgate?' When they replied, 'Yes' I would say to them, 'Have you ever seen those bullet holes in the wall?' and then add 'Do you know what those people were doing? They were fighting for you to get the vote. It is very important to vote and your vote counts as much as that of the Prime Minister.' My mind would go back to the library of the House of Commons where I often met up with Harmer Nicholls MP (Peterborough). He wore cuff links with the figure '3' on them and they had been presented to him by his Constituency Party. The number '3' was his majority at the General Election, which he had won after many recounts. This story, I feel, illustrates the importance of the individual vote. The late Harmer Nicholls was incidentally the father of Audrey, a long-standing figure in 'Coronation Street'.

At the time I was elected to Parliament the motorway was being built around Newport. Part of this project was the excavation work needed to drive through the Brynglas Tunnels. There was a housing development on top of the tunnels and on the evening of 25 May 1966 a lady living there walked into her garden and found herself looking down a hole to the bottom of the tunnels. Families had to be speedily evacuated and some were resident in the Queens Hotel for up to twelve months. Arrangements also had to be made for the storage of their furniture.

Apparently there had been delays in boring the tunnels and this was coupled with complaints from the residents about noise and disturbance caused by blasting. There was a huge question mark as to whether the best way was chosen in taking the by-pass over Brynglas Hill. It was soon revealed that the test borings did not give full enough information about the rock formations. More elaborate borings should have been carried out but the Ministry of Transport did not do this for fear of upsetting the residents. Nevertheless full-scale borings, however inconvenient at the time, would have prevented cracked homes and a lengthy evacuation of families. The public purse had to bear an extra £1 million on account of the delays and there was also the additional cost of keeping families in hotel accommodation.

I paid an early visit to the site with officials from the Department of Transport and discovered that there had been a hole about fifty feet deep and about twenty feet across. A fleet of lorries carrying ready mixed concrete throughout the night filled the hole with 360 cubic yards of concrete. The Government Ministers were naturally concerned about the extra cost of the project and, as I recall, the Welsh Office, acting as agents for the Department of Transport, endeavoured to engage in a minor cost-cutting exercise by making families resident in the Queens Hotel pay for their own food. On the floor of the House of Commons I strongly objected to this proposal, saying that the difficulties that had been caused were not of their own making. The Welsh Office, I am glad to say, quickly backed down.

With Aunt Elizabeth on the House of Commons Terrace.

Residents came to see me at my surgeries at the Civic Centre. They were naturally concerned about the repair work which had to be carried out on their properties. I did my best to help and things were eventually sorted out. One resident was an agent for the Hearts of Oak Friendly Society and, in fairness, he came to see me and said, 'You have done more for me than my solicitor.' It was pleasing to receive such a compliment, particularly as the Brynglas Tunnels difficulty was my first major local exercise as a newly elected Member of Parliament.

CHAPTER 5

'But westward, look, the land is bright'

AFTER MY ELECTION IN March 1966 it became necessary for us to make plans for the future. At the time of my adoption as Parliamentary candidate I promised the General Management Committee that I would return to Gwent and after some consideration we decided to move to Chepstow which was convenient for both Newport and London.

A few months later we left Coventry with sadness but as we drove down to Wales we were reminded of Clough's words 'But westward, look, the land is bright'. For me of course it was a homecoming.

At that time Chepstow was a sleepy little market town with a quality which is special, yet indefinable, to the Marches towns. Until 1966 the only way to cross the Severn estuary was by ferry. These crossings were historic and were very much part of the fabric of life in Chepstow. The opening of the Severn Bridge in 1966 changed Chepstow for ever. The picturesque main street is largely intact, apart from some tasteless developments, but the remainder of the town has changed almost beyond recognition and is still doing so at a rapid pace. It occupies a key position between London, Bristol and South Wales and the motorway network was being put into place in the late sixties. People are attracted to the area by employment prospects in South Wales and the M4 corridor, as it is called. This development is continuing westward following the building of the second Severn crossing. The whole area is convenient for people with interests on both sides of the channel. 1966 saw the first of the housing development and we were among many families, some from different parts of the country, to settle in new houses. The atmosphere was friendly.

I, too, was settling into life in Westminster. It is interesting to compare conditions and services that existed for Members at that time. There was practically no office accommodation available and for the length of a Parliament I worked in the Members' library. This was a pleasant enough environment but there was no base, for as soon as one finished the immediate task, all the papers had to be removed. At that time I employed a part-time Secretary who also worked for the Parliamentary Labour Party. Secretarial allowances were non-existent, as were postal and telephone charges. Rather a disincentive to work! If the *South Wales Argus* wanted me to ring them, the message would be 'Reverse the charges' and the same applied if I were to contact them. All this changed in the early seventies when these charges became free and a secretarial allowance was introduced. In 1970 when our daughters were settled in school, Marion undertook my secretarial work and in 1972 she was made a Magistrate.

We bought a Shetland sheepdog pup from a lady in Tredegar and there was some argument as to his name. Our girls were keen on Pippin, whereas I preferred Rover. Our small daughter Meriel could not get her tongue around Rover and she would say 'Roguer'. Later when something went wrong or was misplaced in the house and no one would own up, Marion and I would say, 'It's that Roguer.' This became a joke and the poor little dog shouldered the blame for all misdeeds.

Our daughter Rosemary took Pippin to the Chepstow Show and entered him in the Dog Section. He had a very good pedigree. There was a lady judge and she happened to place her handbag on the ground, whereupon Pippin cocked his leg up against it. 'Charming,' she said. Pippin was not a prize-winner. He was highly intelligent and we have very fond memories of him. When I was at home I regularly used to take him for a

Sir Geraint Evans and me at the Royal Welsh Show.

walk in the woods adjoining Chepstow racecourse. We called this walk 'The Green Door' which was the entrance to the estate. When we first moved to Chepstow at the end of 1966 it was boarded up because of a major outbreak of foot and mouth disease.

At the bottom of our garden was Welsh Street which provided a sort of back entrance into the town. It was here that visitors invariably got lost. When Pippin and I walked up the street, a car would invariably stop and there would be questions such as 'How do I get to St Pierre?' or 'How do I get to Usk?' One morning a lady stopped to ask directions and then said 'I say, you do look like Sir Geraint Evans.' When I returned to Westminster, I told this story to David Rosser who was then the Political Editor of the *Western Mail*. I seem to recall he used it in his column but he said to me, 'You should have told her that you can sing a good song as well.'

Marion and I regularly visited the Royal Welsh Show at Builth Wells where HTV had a permanent site. Ever present meeting the guests was Sir Geraint Evans who was a director of the company. I came to know him reasonably well and I told him the story of the lady who had told me that he and I were alike in appearance. He was amused and often reminded me of the incident. Apparently on one occasion I was being interviewed on HTV and his brother said to him, 'There's your brother.' Sadly Sir Geraint passed on at a relatively young age and this was a great loss to Opera and to Wales. When we visit Aberaeron, we invariably walk close to his old home, a rather large white house by the estuary close to the sea.

A few days after the General Election victory there was a meeting of the newly elected Parliamentary Labour Party at Church House. I sat next to Maurice Edelman and recognised everyone on the platform with the exception of one white-haired gentleman. I asked who he was and Maurice replied with a smile, 'Roy, that is the Chief Whip, Ted Short'. Ted, I might point out, has always been very friendly to me.

It was then the State opening of Parliament. A colleague John Ellis had won a marginal seat in Bristol. He turned up at the entrance of the House of Commons in his Reliant three-wheeler, whereupon the policeman said, 'I am sorry, Sir, this entrance is for Members only'. John quickly retorted, 'I am a Member.' In the Members' cloakroom each Member has an iron coat hanger, attached to which is a piece of pink ribbon. I asked the attendant what it was for and he said, 'That is for your sword, Sir'. The splendour of the State Opening made me feel a little uneasy but, when I looked at the massed ranks of Members of the Commons, I thought 'what an ordinary looking lot.'

The 1966 General Election had resulted in a Labour

Marion and the girls and our Shetland sheepdog, Pippin.

majority of 98. The campaign had been brilliantly led by Harold Wilson and was based on the slogan 'Building the New Britain'. In retrospect, though, I have often wondered what that Government, with such a large majority, really stood for. The new intake of MPs after the 1966 General Election nevertheless brought into the House of Commons some interesting characters. Stoke-on-Trent had a complete change-over and the three new Members were Jack Ashley, Bob Cant and John Forrester. Before nature dealt him such a cruel blow by depriving him of his hearing, Jack Ashley was most ambitious and following his disability he has shown great courage. Now in his late seventies he still plays an active part in the affairs of the House of Lords.

I became quite friendly with Bob Cant and John Forrester. We spent a lot of time together in the Members' tea room discussing all manner of issues. We maintained this association in meetings, functions and overseas tours with the Roads Group and the Motor Industries Group. I was later to become Chairman of both these bodies. It is interesting to note the difference between these three new Members for Stoke and their predecessors. Jack Ashley and Bob Cant were both Oxford educated and John Forrester was a teacher. One of their predecessors who had retired was Ellis Smith. People like Ellis, who was largely self-taught, were representative of the communities that had sent them to Parliament and they commanded a good deal of respect. One day Ellis Smith was listening to a debate in the Commons and he was not very happy with the nature of the discussion. He rose to his feet to interject and said, 'Mr Speaker, it is all a fackard.' (facade) Another stalwart Member who had retired was Harriet Slater and her claim to fame was that she became the first woman to become a Labour Whip.

Bill Price, a chirpy young journalist had won Rugby. He became a junior Minister but subsequently lost his seat in the debacle of 1983. A native of the Forest of Dean and the son of a miner, Bill returned to his roots and started a weekly newspaper. It covered the Wye Valley, including Chepstow and Caldicot, and I often appeared in its columns.

One of the outstanding Members of the 1966 Parliament, I recall, was Emmanuel Shinwell. He specialised in Parliamentary Questions and although in his mid eighties, he would fling his arms about like a twenty-year old. He represented Easington in County Durham but had originally been a Scottish Member and came to the House of Commons as one of the famous Glasgow rebels. Once there was an incident when a Tory MP is alleged to have told him to go back to Poland. In his youth Shinwell had done some boxing and on this occasion he promptly crossed the floor of the House ready to clobber the offending Member. Another pugilistic encounter was with Stanley Henig, a young academic who had been elected for Lancaster. Shinwell was always bitterly opposed to the Common Market, as it was known at the time, while Henig was what we could call a Euro fanatic. The clash came in the corridor leading from the House of Commons tea room to the Members' lobby. A heated argument broke out between these two protagonists with such an age differential. In the course of the altercation, Shinwell took off his coat and was ready for a full-scale encounter. Another time he went to commiserate with Alec Eadie, a Scottish miners' Member whose wife had recently died. 'Oh, you'll get over it,' he said. 'It has happened to me several times.' On his 100th birthday he made quite a stirring speech in the House of Lords. A truly remarkable man.

During the years I was in the Commons I always sat in the back row just below the gangway. If you sat in the same place when asking a Question or wishing to speak, the Speaker and other hon. Members became accustomed to you being in that particular seat. Sitting immediately in front of me (I could

touch him on the shoulder) was the redoubtable Enoch
Powell. He was a most gifted Parliamentarian but had rather a
steely side to his nature which sometimes came to the fore. In
this connection I recall an incident on 18 January 1978. That
morning the popular Member for Glasgow (Garscadden),
Willie Small, died whilst having breakfast in his hotel. By way
of coincidence that day there were Scottish Questions on the
floor of the Chamber to be followed by a Scotland Bill. Each
Member as he rose to speak prefaced his remarks by paying
tribute to their departed colleague. On 20 January there
appeared on the Order Paper an Early Day Motion (No 194)
standing in the name of Mr J. Enoch Powell and reading as
follows:

> That this House deplores the abuse of Question Time on 18th
> January so as further to erode the long-standing and salutary
> practice of this House, whereby, except in a jealously limited
> category of outstanding eminence, the decease of an honourable
> Member is the occasion for no formal tribute other than Mr
> Speaker's unvarying formula.

This Early Day Motion was a strictly accurate interpretation
of the procedures but seemed to lack a bit of sympathy and
humanity. This was the viewpoint of some forty MPs who
signed an amendment to the original motion to the effect that
they welcomed the opportunity to pay tribute to their late
colleague.

Another long serving Member is Tom Cox (Tooting), who
has become quite a character of the House. During the Second
World War he was a Bevin boy and as such worked as an
electrician in the North Celynen Colliery between Newbridge
and Crumlin in Gwent. He stayed close by with relatives in
Oakdale. Tom's Parliamentary seat was at one stage rather
marginal and at the 1979 General Election his opponent was
(Sir) Fergus Montgomery. Tom Cox recalls – 'In the Election

campaign Fergus Montgomery went to speak to the Tooting Conservative Ladies Luncheon Club and said how wonderful Margaret (Thatcher) was as their Leader, what a superb Prime Minister she would become and that she would follow all the policies that the Party was then committed to. To ensure that Margaret became the Prime Minister, it was essential to win seats like Tooting. He closed by saying, "Ladies, I am delighted to be here with you today but as I close my remarks I have a slogan that I give you and I want you to use this slogan wherever you are in the coming weeks in the run-up to the General Election. Use it at every opportunity and the slogan ladies is very, very clear and it is 'Cox out in Tooting'." He told me this story himself and he said he expected after what he thought was a brilliant speech to hear his final comments received with rapturous applause but instead there were looks of disgust from the Tooting ladies who really thought, "What on earth does he think he has just said to us? How disgraceful. How disgusting. Why ever did we choose this fellow to come and speak to us today?"'

One of the features of the 1966 Parliament was that so many of our new entrants who had won seats from the Tories were in the House for only one session. Most of them I have never seen since. I note, though, that the young Stanley Henig is now a Professor, while Dr Hugh Grey, the former Member for Yarmouth, went out to India to do some charity work. Then there was Ben Whittaker (Hampstead) with an impeccable speaking voice. I was surprised to meet his wife recently as a newly ennobled life peer. The political swing is pretty relentless but I formed the impression that many of them were very clever and able people but at the same time they lacked a bit of political 'nous' and this contributed to their downfall.

Of course one of the great characters in the House today is Dennis Skinner, the so-called Beast of Bolsover, a name and description given to him by Nicholas Soames (Crawley), a

grandson of Sir Winston Churchill. Dennis tends to wear the
hair shirt and his stance on principle would never allow him to
'pair' with a member of the Opposition. One evening a Tory
MP came up to him and said, 'Is it all right to go home,
Dennis?' This was a way of asking if they could pair in the
event of a vote. Dennis said, 'Aye, OK'. Later in the evening
Dennis had two more similar requests and each time he gave
the same reply. The following morning there was quite a
hullabaloo. Tory Whips charged into the Labour Whips' office
asking what sort of game they were playing. Needless to say,
ever afterwards no Tory MP invited Dennis Skinner to 'pair'.

Once Dennis came to speak to my General Management
Committee during the closing stages of the Callaghan
administration He lambasted all and sundry and in the course
of his remarks mentioned that 'Roy and I have voted against
the Government fifty-seven times.' Present at the meeting was
a reporter from the *South Wales Argus* and Dennis's remarks on
voting were duly reported in the columns of the newspaper the
following evening. Of course I had not voted against the
Government as Dennis had intimated so I wrote a letter to the
Argus Editor indicating that my good friend Dennis might
have got a little bit carried away. I had possibly abstained once
or twice on issues about which I felt strongly, but I had never
voted against a Labour Government. I must say I am one of
Dennis's admirers. He has a very sharp mind and tries at all
times to speak up for ordinary people. Sadly there are so few
like him today.

I served for many years in the House of Commons before
proceedings were televised. This development was inevitable
but has not enhanced the standing and prestige of Parliament
in the country. It has generated sound bites and synthetic
politics whilst often trivialising major issues. To some extent it
might have improved the behaviour of MPs in the Chamber
because Members are conscious of being televised. During all-

night sittings in years gone by, I have seen Members sprawled all over the place and the benches in front of where the TV cameras are now located was a favourite twilight zone. One comical incident I recall before proceedings were televised related to a popular Yorkshire mining MP who had quite a respectable image in his constituency. His weakness, however, was that immediately he got on the train on a Monday morning he went straight to the bar and by the time he arrived in London he was well away. His condition was made worse when he soon drifted along to the Strangers' Bar in the House of Commons. One day he stumbled into the Chamber and was soon slumped on the floor between the benches. Sitting in the aisle above was Ray Powell (Ogmore) and in the Chair was the then Deputy Speaker, George Thomas.* A Tory MP was making some rather outlandish remarks when the MP in a horizontal position chirped up 'Fooking right, too.' With that the Deputy Speaker wagged his finger, like the teacher he was, calling Ray Powell up to the Chair. They were of course both from the Rhondda and knew each other well. George said to Ray, 'I know what you said' and the protestations of innocence by the Member for Ogmore were of little avail.

The Party's manifesto in 1964 had stated Labour's objectives as 'A New Britain – mobilising resources of technology under a national plan, harnessing our national wealth in brains, our genius for scientific invention and medical discovery, reversing the decline of thirteen wasted years; affording a new opportunity to equal, and if possible, surpass the roaring progress of other Western powers while Tory Britain has moved sideways, backwards but seldom forwards. The country needs fresh and virile leadership. Labour is ready.'

There was soon, however, news that the Balance of Payments deficit had risen to such a high level that a quick

---

*Subsequently Speaker of the House and later Viscount Tonypandy.

decision was required about the future of sterling. Senior Treasury and Bank of England officials quickly made it clear that the economic policies of the Conservatives during their last months in office amounted to criminal negligence. When the Labour Government was first elected in October 1964 with a wafer-thin majority it was soon faced with serious financial and economic problems. The election had followed thirteen continuous years of Tory rule. Harold Macmillan had stood down in 1963 allegedly on health grounds but his Government had been seriously buffeted, particularly by the Profumo scandal. There was an almighty scramble for the leadership with Rab Butler the favourite, but Lord Hailsham (Quintin Hogg) also threw his hat into the ring. Ultimately the traditional 'old boy' network of the Tory Party prevailed and HM The Queen sent for Lord Home (Sir Alec Douglas Home) to charge him with forming the next Government. In the event he went right to the wire, staying in office until the end of the five year term.

During this time the Shadow Chancellor, James Callaghan, was fearful of making criticism of the economy, believing that it might damage sterling. He was concerned, too, that pressure on sterling could create problems for an incoming Labour Government and eventually lead to devaluation.

Reginald Maudling, the Chancellor of the Exchequer in the Home Government, had made a headlong and barely controlled expansionist drive which quickly got out of hand. Lord Cromer, the Governor of the Bank of England, wrote to the Treasury on 18 August 1965 stating that for some time he had felt 'considerable misgivings about the direction in which our financial affairs are going'. He complained that he had asked the Chancellor to convey his misgivings to the Prime Minister but this had not been done. The top civil servant, Sir William Armstrong, had already spelt out his concern indicating that 'the balance of payments is very bad'.

Some years later James Callaghan, who had been appointed Chancellor of the Exchequer, told us at the Welsh table in the Members' tea room that his Conservative predecessor, Reginald Maudling, came right away to his room and apologised for the mess he had got the economy into. James Callaghan is a very able politician but he was not a trained economist and during this period he was under tremendous pressure. I heard a report that he actually lost two and a half stone in weight due to the burden he was carrying.

Harold Wilson, the Prime Minister, who had held a major economic post in the Attlee Government, was insistent that devaluation was the option to be avoided and a quick decision was taken by senior Ministers to hold to the existing parity. I often found it interesting to recall the concern about the Balance of Payments which seemed to have dominated the 1966-70 Parliament. Even in the factories up and down the country there was animated discussion about this subject. Today Governments pay little more than lip service to it and for the man in the street it is a non-event.

Despite the firm decision to hold to the existing parity of sterling, the economy continued to deteriorate. This soon had an effect on Party morale, both amongst MPs and supporters throughout the country. Such disenchantment led to the Government losing by-elections in what had normally been regarded as safe Labour seats. Likewise it fuelled nationalist aspirations both in Wales and Scotland.

Eventually in November 1967 we had the inevitable devaluation, although both Wilson and Callaghan had done everything possible to avoid such a development. At this stage Callaghan and Roy Jenkins exchanged jobs, the former moving to the Home Office and the latter taking over at the Treasury. Devaluation provided some respite for sterling but this did not last long. A few months later pressure resumed and the Prime Minister's difficulties were not helped by the volatility of the

Foreign Secretary, George Brown. George had an inbuilt resentment of Wilson who in 1963 had beaten him in the leadership contest following the death of Hugh Gaitskell. Both issues came to a head on Thursday 14th March – the personality clash together with the big losses of reserves.

In the afternoon and early evening, the Commons had been debating a guillotine motion on the Transport Bill, which was a major piece of legislation. Richard Crossman was Leader of the House and Barbara Castle the sponsoring Minister. Among the provisions of this Bill was the introduction of the breathalyser. Nowadays, this device is widely accepted as necessary to prevent carnage on the roads but this was the not the case at the time. Motorists tended to think of the legislation as an infringement of their personal liberty. Guillotine motions are brought about through delay and sometimes deadlock in Standing Committee. They are always objected to by the Opposition, whichever party is in power at the time, but it is merely a case of the pot calling the kettle black. In this instance the motion was carried and the House moved on to other business.

Meanwhile much was happening outside the Chamber over the threat to sterling and both the Prime Minister and the Chancellor were forced to take emergency action. In the urgent and important discussions which took place, the Foreign Secretary would normally have been present but it was alleged by the Prime Minister that he could not be found. Later, Brown hotly denied that there had been any realistic attempt to find him.

While going around the corridors of the Commons late that evening I picked up a chance remark that George Brown had resigned. I mentioned this to a very right-wing AEU sponsored Member, Cyril Bence, who, despite representing a Scottish seat, actually came from Newport. He said bluntly, 'No, there's nothing for him to resign for.' I was a new, young, and inexperienced Member and I said to myself, 'Hughes, why don't you shut up?' In the event what I had gathered proved to be true. Later that evening George Brown was virtually carried out of the tea room by his brother Ron and another Whip. During the hullabaloo Brown, the Foreign Secretary, was questioning whether the Prime Minister's parents had ever been married. This was high drama for a lad from the mining valleys of South Wales.

It appears that about 11.00 p.m. there was a request from Washington 'to close down the London Gold Pool'. The Prime Minister, together with the Chancellor and O'Brien, the Governor of the Bank of England, agreed on the need to declare the next day a Bank Holiday, in order to shut down the London foreign exchange market. The Prime Minister authorised the convening of a meeting of the Privy Council which was necessary before such an announcement could be made. In the event only the Prime Minister, the Chancellor, Roy Jenkins, and Peter Shore attended. Meanwhile George Brown, the Foreign Secretary, was furious about what had happened and firmly believed that Harold Wilson had endeavoured to exclude him from these important decisions. Wilson maintained that he had been trying for an hour and a quarter to contact him. Other senior Ministers, however, also complained about being by-passed. George Brown tendered his resignation and this time it was a point of no return. The Prime Minister accepted it and Michael Stewart became the new Foreign Secretary.

The Tories in the Commons were in uproar because they expected another devaluation. I recall a rather eerie atmosphere prevailing after the House had been adjourned. Crossman, Leader of the Commons, phoned the Prime Minister to let him know the situation and that he and the Chancellor were needed to provide reassurance. At 3.15 a.m. Wilson and Jenkins went over to face a packed House. The confrontation went well for both, who acquitted themselves admirably.

Later I recall leaving the Commons with Cliff Williams (Abertillery) to catch the first underground train to Paddington at 6.30 a.m. Lacking any real inside knowledge of events we were both convinced that the Government was going to fall. In the event, Wilson and his beleaguered administration soldiered on. I served for thirty-one years in the House of Commons but Thursday, 14 March, 1968 was the most momentous day (and night).

CHAPTER 6

National and International Problems

A MAJOR FEATURE OF THE 1966 Parliament was the rise of nationalism in Scotland and Wales. In November 1967 Winnie Ewing won Hamilton in a by-election and proclaimed that Scotland was back on the map. Eventually she had a dozen colleagues and this was the time of the discovery of North Sea oil. Whenever the word oil was mentioned in the Chamber, there was regularly a chant from the nationalists: 'Scottish oil'. Their glory, though, did not last long, for they almost all lost their seats in the subsequent General Election. Since then, of course, they have regrouped and are still a major force in Scottish politics.

In Wales support for the new Labour Government with its huge Parliamentary majority quickly turned sour. People there had long memories for they could not bring themselves to vote Tory. They recalled the days of the industrial depression in the 1920s and 30s when people were starving and the Means Test was the order of the day. Arguments could still he heard of Churchill's alleged militaristic encounter with the miners in the Rhondda valley early in the century. As a result of the reluctance of people to support the alternative major national party, the Conservatives in Wales, the vacuum was filled by the Welsh Nationalist Party, Plaid Cymru.

In 1951 Lady Megan Lloyd George had lost her Anglesey seat to Cledwyn Hughes, a local solicitor. By the mid fifties the Liberal Party was very much in decline and so the daughter of World War One Prime Minister threw in her lot with Labour. She was joined by a number of other Liberals, including

Dingle Foot of the famous west country family and, of course, a brother of Michael. Lady Megan was soon back in the House of Commons as the Labour Member for Carmarthen. In February 1957 she won a by-election following the death of Sir Rhys Hopkins Morris. She defeated her Liberal opponent in a remarkably high poll of 87.5 per cent. By the time of the 1966 General Election Lady Megan was suffering from cancer and fought the election virtually on her death bed. She won a convincing victory, though, trouncing her nearest rival, H. Davies, a Liberal, by a majority of 9,233. Following her death a by-election was called for 14 July 1966 and all four major parties in Wales again contested the seat. The only change in the line-up was that Gwilym Prys Davies, a Pontypridd solicitor, was now the Labour candidate. Some years earlier he had been a member of the Nationalist Party.

The fortunes of the newly elected Labour Government had quickly taken a downward turn. In his message to the Conservative candidate Mr Simon Day, Mr Edward Heath, Party Leader, said, 'The Labour Party is now split asunder over Vietnam, is deeply divided over policy East of Suez and is so torn apart over the Prices and Incomes Bill that a senior Cabinet Minister has resigned.'

Mr Enoch Powell came down to Carmarthen to support his Party's candidate but the Liberals were expected to be the main challenge to Labour. Coming up on the rails, though, was Mr Gwynfor Evans, President of Plaid Cymru, who had previously tried seven times to enter Parliament. It was noticeable that he had pushed up his Party's vote in the constituency from 2000 in 1959 to 7416 in the March 1966 General Election. After a most keenly fought election Mr Gwynfor Evans won a stunning victory. It was a major blow for Labour and since then Plaid Cymru has been a major threat in Wales.

Back in the House of Commons I sat at the Welsh table in the Members' tea room where the rather elderly group of

Labour Members were dumbfounded. They had controlled affairs for so long and such a major turnaround was difficult to take in. I recall one former miners' official saying, 'What will we do if he comes and sits here?' It was rather a farcical situation.

At the time there was an ethos in Wales over the language. In the heavily populated area of South East Wales, Welsh was scarcely spoken at all and elected representatives did little, if anything, to promote the language. On the contrary they were quite antagonistic towards it. It was as if the working class culture was afraid of what had once been the native tongue in the area. Afraid, too, that a Welsh-speaking elite could take control of affairs and this, at least to a limited extent, has actually taken place. For myself I got on rather well with the new nationalist Member whom I found to be a charming person. My basic loyalty to Labour was not, however, undermined. Gwynfor Evans proclaimed that Wales now had an independent voice in the House and more high drama was to follow.

One Thursday evening in December 1966 I sat at the bottom of the library in the Commons waiting for the ten o'clock vote. Sitting next to me was the Member for Rhondda West, Iorrie Thomas, and when the division bell rang he rose from his seat and said, 'Which way shall we go?', meaning which direction shall we take to get to the division lobby. On the Saturday I was travelling to Cardiff by car with my long-standing friends from Blackwood. We were on our way to a rugby match. The car radio was switched on for the one o'clock news and the announcement was made that Mr Iorrie Thomas, Member of Parliament for Rhondda West, had died. Needless to say I was shocked at the news, having been with him so recently. He had represented the constituency for seventeen years and was very popular in the House of Commons. His majority in the March 1966 General Election was over 16,000.

The Secretary of the Rhondda West Constituency Labour Party was Alec Jones, a teacher who had fairly recently returned from London to his native valley. At the funeral of the constituency's Member of Parliament, Alec told me later that in the churchyard he was approached by a London MP and his wife. The MP proceeded to point out what an excellent Member his wife would be for the Rhondda. He stressed his Welsh roots and asked that the lady should be given every consideration. Needless to say, such effrontery was given short shrift.

For the impending by-election the Nationalist Party quickly put in place its electoral machinery. Even in the early stages of the campaign they were forecasting a second Carmarthen. Their election agent Mr Cennard Davies quoted in the *Western Mail* on 7 February 1967 said, 'Even in what are considered Labour households, we have been promised firm support at the election and the electorate appear to consider this election as a straight fight between Labour and Plaid Cymru.'

This was fighting talk in what for generations had been considered a Labour stronghold. Meanwhile there were little local difficulties in the selection of a Labour candidate to fight this important by-election. There was talk of cliques, anonymous letters and much nastiness in this famous and historic valley. In the past, there would have been no doubt as to who got the nomination, for traditionally it had been a miners' seat. In 1885 the legendary William Abraham 'Mabon' had been elected with a pledge to fight for the working man and he served thirty-five years in Parliament. Subsequently, with the growth in population, Rhondda was split into two constituencies, East and West. The economic structure of the Rhondda, however, was changing fast and the miners now had nothing like the support they used to command. Pit closures had reduced their voting power and their influence. Likewise their worthy candidate Mr Will Woods did not appear to have the charisma to fill the uncommitted with the conviction that he was the man to save the Rhondda. People were dissatisfied with social conditions and rapidly escalating unemployment. At this time 1,000 people were leaving the Rhondda each year.

In the Commons there were serious discussions as to who should be selected, particularly between Elfed Davies who represented Rhondda East, and George Thomas who, although representing Cardiff West, was still very much concerned about his native Rhondda where his famous mother (Mam) still lived. I quickly gathered that they were most anxious for Alec Jones to be selected.

Five nominees were placed on the short list: Ken Griffin, the local officer of the Electricians Trade Union, Les Thomas, Chairman of the Constituency Party, Tal Lloyd of the AEU, John Reynolds, a Cardiff lecturer, and Alec Jones. In those days it was not at all unusual to have all male short lists. An ambitious lady was Mrs Sylvia Jones, Secretary of the Rhondda Borough Labour Party. This is the body which co-ordinates the East and West Parties although each constituency jealously safeguards its own autonomy. Mrs Jones is quoted as saying that she was bitter about her exclusion from the short list.

At the time she had three young children, and one Branch Secretary is alleged to have said to her, 'What if you have another baby?' Others asked her, 'If you went into Parliament, who would look after the children?' These exchanges illustrate the attitude prevailing at the time about women becoming full-time politicians. Things have changed so much and at the 1997 General Election over a hundred women Labour MPs were elected to the Commons.

In the event Alec Jones was selected but before taking his seat in Westminster he had to fight a very difficult and close election. The poll took place on Thursday 9 March 1967 and the Labour nominee beat the Plaid Cymru candidate by 2,306 votes. This was a marked change from the 'safe as houses' seat

which Iorrie Thomas had won in March 1966 with a majority
of over 16,000. It was a bitterly fought campaign and the two
principal parties did their utmost to secure victory. The
proceedings at the count and when the result was announced
were quite acrimonious and this had also been a feature at the
earlier Carmarthen by-election. Mr Emrys Jones, the
experienced Welsh Regional Secretary of the Labour Party, was
so concerned about what might happen that he advised Alec
Jones's wife to stay away from the count. After he had taken up
his seat Alec turned out to be an excellent MP and a worthy
representative of the Rhondda.

Some years later the Boundary Commission recommended
that, due to a fall in population, Rhondda should revert once
again to being one constituency. This was to involve a rather
painful selection contest between Elfed Davies, who had
represented Rhondda East for fifteen years, and the more
recently elected Member for Rhondda West. In the event
Alec Jones was selected and later became a Junior Minister.
His colleague Elfed Davies was made a life peer. Alec was
ambitious but unfortunately his health did not hold out and he
suffered a serious heart attack. I recall that when the majority
of the Callaghan Government in the seventies was on a knife
edge, Alec was carried in on a stretcher to the room next to
mine. There is a procedure in the Commons that in the case of
a sick Member provided he is on the premises, a Whip can nod
him through the division lobby. Alec made a partial recovery
but he died soon afterwards. After his death Alan Rogers, a
Euro Member, became MP for the Rhondda. I had close links
with Alec Jones because for a short time we shared the same
room. Ray Gunter had become Minister of Labour (the bed of
nails as he called it) in 1964 and as a Cabinet Minister he
seldom used his room in the Commons. Elfed Davies
(Rhondda East) was Gunter's Parliamentary Private Secretary
and he took over the room. After Alec Jones (Rhondda West)

was elected, he shared it with Elfed but when Rhondda became one seat Alec asked me to share the room with him and after he died I was there on my own for about twenty-five years. It was a most convenient room bordering on to the Speaker's Court, close to the division lobbies, Members' tea room and other important facilities.

Ness Edwards died in 1968 after representing Caerphilly for twenty-nine years. After their victory in Carmarthen and a near miss in the Rhondda, Plaid Cymru were cock-a-hoop. Their selected candidate for the by-election was Dr Phil Williams, an academic who came from Tredegar. Labour broke with tradition by selecting as their candidate Fred Evans, a local headmaster. The miners' nominee was Lance Rogers, a miners' agent who had turned down a scholarship to Oxford to take part in the Spanish Civil War on the side of the Republicans. When he failed to get selected, Dai Francis, Secretary of the South Wales Miners, said, 'We are extremely disappointed.'

During the campaign when I canvassed in the area I was amazed at the support for the Nationalists in what had been over many years such a strong Labour area. Some electors with Labour posters in their windows took them down and replaced them with those of Plaid Cymru. In the event on polling day, 18 July 1968, a Labour majority of over 21,000 in 1966 was reduced to 1,874. Throughout the intervening years the 'Nats' as many in South Wales refer to them, have continued to be a threat to Labour. They are now, too, a major force in Local Government and in 1999 won control of Caerphilly Borough Council and that of Rhondda Cynon Taff. This is besides being the principal opposition party in the newly created Welsh Assembly.

Prior to the Second World War Vietnam was part of the French Indo-Chinese empire but then it was occupied by the Japanese. After the war France attempted to reassert its authority but was eventually driven out in 1954. The country was then divided between the communist Democratic Republic in the North and the 'State of Vietnam' in the South. Civil war broke out and from 1961 onwards America became heavily involved on the side of the South which was ruled by a corrupt dictatorial regime. Vast amounts of American aid were poured in, together with ever-increasing numbers of military advisors.

From 1964 onwards US aircraft bombarded the North and by 1968 over 500,000 US troops were involved. American commanders threatened to bomb the Vietnamese 'back to the stone age'. Atrocities were widespread, symbolised by the My Lai incident. Charlie Company, a unit of the American Division's 11th Infantry Brigade, had been in Vietnam for just over three months. They were young Americans with an average age of about twenty. On 16 March 1968, they entered an undefended village on the coast of Central Vietnam and murdered about 500 old men, women and children in cold blood. The killings took place, part maniacally, part methodically, over a period of four hours. The atrocities included rape, sodomy, mutilations and unimaginable random cruelties.

This cruel war led to mass protests all over the world but particularly in America itself. The University campuses were alive with dissent. Lyndon Baines Johnson, who had taken over as President following the assassination of John Kennedy in November 1963, was trying to prevail on Harold Wison to commit at least a token British force to Vietnam, as had happened in the Korea War a decade or so earlier. Harold Wilson was in a difficult position. On the one hand the Government was desperate for American aid to support sterling, but the Prime Minister realised that if British forces were sent to Vietnam all hell would break loose in the Parliamentary Labour Party and in the Labour Movement throughout the country. Student protest was only likely to gather apace. Wilson did not give way to the American President but instead used soothing words and tried, albeit in a limited way, to find a peaceful solution. There were regular rows in the Parliamentary Labour Party over Vietnam with vocal Members like Eric Heffer, Stanley Orme and Norman Atkinson prominent in the attack and opposing what was seen to be American aggression. I supported the protests, particularly by signing Early Day Motions which appeared on the order paper of the House of Commons.

Despite huge efforts American action failed and in 1973 their troops were withdrawn and hostilities ceased in 1975 when the North's victory was completed with the capture of Saigon (renamed Ho Chi Minh City). At this time a group of Viet Cong partisans came to a committee room in the House of Commons and were greeted as heroes by Labour MPs.

In June 1968 after three years of deliberating came the report of the Royal Commission on Trade Unions and Employers' Associations under the Chairmanship of Lord Donovan. The Prime Minister, Harold Wilson, was hoping to use trade union reform to streamline the economy and to help regain credibility with the electorate. Two months before Donovan, he had replaced the unpopular Minister of Labour Ray Gunter, with Barbara Castle and the Ministry under her direction was given a new grandiose title 'Employment and Productivity'. There was an added responsibility for incomes policy, which was taken from the Department of Economic Affairs.

Barbara Castle had begun her Ministerial career in 1964 as Minister for Overseas Development with a seat in the Cabinet. She moved to the Department of Transport where she introduced a mammoth Transport Bill which was intended to help bring about an integrated transport system and which had long been the rallying cry in Labour's ranks. The investment, however, was not made available to bring about the fundamental changes that were necessary to implement such a policy.

In September 1966, my first year in the House of Commons, we had the opening of the Severn Bridge by HM the Queen. What was noticeable then was that two ladies were taking centre stage – Her Majesty the Queen and a thrusting Minister Barbara Castle who had no intention of taking a back seat. When Barbara Castle moved to her new Ministry she was replaced by Richard Marsh and I seem to recall that he toned down some of the provisions contained in what became known as the 1968 Transport Act. The Member for Blackburn, though, was now at the height of her powers and in January 1969 she brought out a White Paper called 'In Place of Strife'. The Prime Minister was apparently very pleased with this new document but it was later to cause terrible dissension in the Cabinet and throughout the ranks of the Labour Movement.

The Trade Unions were bitter about some of the proposals. They felt they were being put in a straitjacket, for the whole intent was to regulate Union behaviour. The new Minister could impose pre-strike ballots and order a twenty-eight day conciliation pause. An Industrial Board was to be established to impose fines should there be non-compliance with the new rules. Apart from the Unions, many MPs including myself thought at the time that this was hardly the sort of legislation to be expected from a Labour Government. In the event the document caused so much dissension that it came closer than any other issue, domestic or foreign, to forcing the Prime Minister's resignation. He believed implicitly in the proposals contained in the White Paper but the Home Secretary James Callaghan was basically opposed. In the ensuing political warfare that took place supporters of Roy Jenkins thought this was their opportunity to oust Harold Wilson and put their man into Number Ten.

Meanwhile, though, Callaghan realised that the issue of

trade union reform gave him the opportunity to get large sections of the Movement loyal to him. This would be very helpful in any future Labour Party fight. It was this jockeying for position, with the Jenkinites waiting to pounce and Callaghan confident of considerable support from large sections of the Movement as a whole, that probably saved Harold Wilson. These two factions tended to cancel each other out. At least Callaghan took a principled stand and had made a realistic assessment of the support he could expect from the Unions and the 120 or so MPs they sponsored.

In the torrid atmosphere that prevailed there were other major players. To try and stem persistent indiscipline in the Parliamentary Party, the Prime Minister had earlier appointed the arch right-winger Bob Mellish as Chief Whip. John Silkin whom he replaced tended to be left of centre. This change did not go down well with the left of the Party. I recall the meeting in the Grand Committee Room of the Parliamentary Labour Party with Michael Foot on his feet denouncing the new appointment and this was well after Douglas Houghton the Chairman had banged his gavel on the table and declared the meeting closed.

It came as something of a surprise to Wilson, therefore, when Mellish in his usual blunt manner told the Cabinet that in no way could the proposals contained in the White Paper 'In Place of Strife' be got through the House of Commons. The Prime Minister was also to be disappointed with the lack of support from the younger members of his Cabinet, namely Judith Hart, Peter Shore and Richard Marsh. They all opposed the measure. Barbara Castle also opposed Mellish's appointment and actually sent a letter of resignation to the Prime Minister, believing it to be an attack on the Left to which she was still nominally attached. In the event Wilson quickly talked her out of it.

On 3 March 1969 in a debate on the White Paper fifty-five

MPs (including myself) voted against and some forty abstained. This was a rebellion of major proportions. Three weeks later the National Executive Committee added its own opposition, with Callaghan actually opposing the policy of the Government of which he was a member. What should the Prime Minister do? Sack him? Here it is interesting to note the attitude of the then Anthony Wedgwood Benn. He argued for strict adherence to the principle of Cabinet collective responsibility. Benn made clear his point of view and suggested that the Prime Minister should write to Callaghan in the following terms – 'Dear Jim, As you are no longer prepared to defend Government policy in public, I assume you have resigned.' Wilson realised, though, that he was no longer in a strong enough position to sack Callaghan and the strife continued. Marcia Williams summed up the situation, when 'In Place of Strife' dominated discussion, as 'the most unpleasant, disastrous and dramatic of all time in Downing Street.'

Barbara Castle was coming under almost intolerable pressure and she demonstrated this around the corridors of the House. I recall an incident involving John Horner MP (Oldbury and Halesowen) an ex-Communist who had become far more moderate in his viewpoint. Before coming to the House of Commons he had spent many years as General Secretary of the Fire Brigades Trade Union. One day he tried to give Barbara a bit of useful advice based on his many years of experience in the Trade Union movement. In response she became almost hysterical. There were reports that Wilson, too, was cracking under the strain. The Cabinet came out two to one against his proposal that he could tell the TUC that either they must alter their rules or the penal clause would be made law. At this stage it seems that Jenkins changed sides, which virtually settled the issue and left Wilson and Barbara Castle even more isolated.

On 18 June the Prime Minister met the General Council of the TUC and recklessly threatened them with the legislation which the Cabinet had already turned down. The Union leaders were shrewd enough to realise that the Prime Minister was in a weak position but they also recognised that if he resigned they might be faced with Roy Jenkins who had even less sympathy for their cause.

I recall the conclusion of this turbulent period. The Parliamentary Labour Party's Trade Union Group were meeting on the Committee floor of the House of Commons. It was a packed meeting presided over by Victor Yates, a rather jovial Birmingham Member, who had taken over the Chairmanship after Ness Edwards's death. We were told that the Prime Minister would be arriving soon and eventually he appeared, accompanied by Victor Feather who had earlier replaced George Woodcock as General Secretary of the TUC following the latter's retirement. They almost ran into the room, huffing and puffing, so to speak. It was quickly but rather gravely announced by the Prime Minister that 'a solemn and binding undertaking had been given by the Unions, which had the same status as the 1939 Bridlington Declaration on inter-union disputes'. The formula was the brainchild of Hugh Scanlon, President of the Engineers' Union, and Jack Jones, General Secretary of the TGWU. They were both to play a major part in trade union and governmental affairs in the immediate years ahead. There were to be no changes in TUC rules but Wilson and Castle convinced themselves that they had scored a victory and resignations had been avoided. It was to some extent a cosmetic exercise but nevertheless the TUC kept its undertaking to intervene in unofficial disputes, greatly reducing the number of strikes as a result.

The Prime Minister proved to be a survivor. In the spring and early summer of 1969 he had been under grave threat, with widespread speculation as to whether he could survive until the General Election. Now the tide turned as the economy began to recover. The benefits of devaluation were beginning to show and a greater spirit of optimism soon emerged amongst the beleaguered ranks of the Parliamentary Labour Party. There is nothing like an approaching General Election to bring unity in the ranks of the Labour Party.

CHAPTER 7

Maiden Speech

I MADE MY MAIDEN SPEECH ON 25 May 1966 and it was
during the Second Reading of the Finance Bill. The Speaker
at the time was Dr Horace King.★ I went up to his chair and
said, 'Mr Speaker, I would like to make my Maiden Speech,'
and he replied, 'When Margaret Thatcher sits down you are on.
Good luck.'

The future Prime Minister, I should point out, was at the
time the number two Treasury Spokesman for the Conservatives in opposition. In my speech I pointed out that 'we were
anxiously awaiting the decision of the Minister of Transport
(Barbara Castle) on the future organisation and development
of dock facilities in the Bristol Channel.' The City of Bristol
which owned the local docks was anxious to develop a major
new ports complex which some of us felt would be highly
damaging to the South Wales ports. Barbara Castle refused to
allow it to go ahead and this decision was reaffirmed by
Richard Marsh when he took over as Minister of Transport.
He said, 'I reject the scheme because the discounted cash flow
is insufficient and there is no industrial hinterland.' Again on
the 8 July he pointed out, 'If I were a Bristolian I would have
some doubts about a project which would be such a charge
on public funds as this one.' These proved to be very wise
words. The Conservatives, however, realised that there were at
least two marginal seats to be won in Bristol and they
announced that if elected in the 1970 General Election they

★Later Lord Mowbray King.

95

would introduce the necessary legislation to allow Bristol to go ahead.

Since entering Parliament I had taken an interest in ports and became Secretary of the Parliamentary Labour Party's Ports Group. The people of Newport had always been proud of their docks for they tended to mirror the history of the town. I was rather proud, too, when I was invited to join the Newport Docks Branch of the Transport & General Workers Union. This meant transferring my membership from the Midlands and the 5/359 Branch which I had served as Secretary for seven years. Because of my interest I was able to spotlight the 'Bristol' issue and Welsh MPs became very concerned about the Conservative opposition proposals. This was particularly so when the Tories formed the next Government under Ted Heath. A Welsh Grand Committee debate was called for. This body included all Welsh MPs plus four English Tories to obtain a better balance because for quite some years the Labour Party had always had a big majority amongst Welsh Members. In the debate I was appointed to 'wind up' for the Opposition and George Thomas, the Shadow Secretary of State for Wales, was to open the debate. He was a very colourful figure and really went out of his way to project his friendly and genial nature. His first Ministerial post had been in 1964 when Harold Wilson, the Prime Minister, made him a Junior Minister at the Home Office. The story is told that one of his first appointments was a visit to Cardiff Jail in the City where he had represented the West constituency since 1945. On entering the prison complex, a prisoner came up to him and said, 'George, what are you in for?'

My speech was well received and I bitterly attacked the Bristol proposals and Welsh Ministers and Conservative MPs for supporting them. Afterwards George Thomas said to me, 'Well done. There will be other opportunities.'

By this time the Corporation of Bristol had scaled down its

original Portbury scheme, which would have cost £27 million to accommodate very large ships. Now they proposed building a dock to take ships up to 65,000 tons, which was regarded as being neither one thing nor the other, or, as my Northern wife would say, 'Neither nowt nor summat'. Contemporary thinking called for docks to cater for ships of 100,000 tons and over, or for ships of 30,000 tons or less. Mr Tom Roberts, the colourful Ports Director in South Wales, poured ridicule on the scheme, as did the Newport Docks Manager Mr Vernon Snow. The Ports Management had the full backing of the dockers and in Newport Jimmy Heaven, their leader, left no one in any doubt where they stood. The Heaven family were a big force in the Docks and at this time no fewer than five of them were employed there.

In the 1970 General Election, however, the Conservative Party was returned to power and the Prime Minister Ted Heath appointed a West Country member, John Peyton, as Minister of Transport. He was determined to honour the promise the Conservatives had made at the General Election. On 7 November 1970 he gave the go-ahead for the revised project. Ironically the National Ports Council also lent their support for the rather inane reason that other ports had been allowed to get on with their new schemes. The logic of this argument was quite incomprehensible. Thus on 1st July 1971 on the floor of the House of Commons, we had the Second Reading debate on the Bristol Corporation (West Dock) Bill. Its provisions were to construct a new system called West Dock on land across the River Avon opposite Avonmouth. The estimated cost was £12-£13 million and the land had been purchased by Bristol Corporation way back in 1959. In the debate I pleaded with them to 'think again' but there was no going back. When the vote came we were heavily defeated.

The building of the Portbury Docks went ahead and HM the Queen opened them on 8 August 1997. That, however, was only the beginning of the story because for years the new docks were a huge loss-maker. The project cost the ratepayers of Bristol millions of pounds as the overheads must have been prohibitive. Bristol Corporation tried to sell the docks but there was no buyer. I believe that if they had had the opportunity they would have given them away; the City of Bristol certainly paid dearly for its civic pride. In was in August 1991 that a private buyer was eventually found.

When I was first elected it was interesting to view the South Wales Labour contingent which contained many elderly former officials of the Miners' Union. They congregated at the Welsh Table in the Tea Room of the Commons. To me as a newcomer the presiding member seemed to be Ness Edwards, who represented Caerphilly but was a native of Abertillery. He smoked Craven A cigarettes and I recall he always wore an Anthony Eden Homburg hat, all so different from Welsh MPs today. Clement Attlee in 1945 had made him Postmaster General in his Government. After the General Election of 1964 he became Chairman of the then most powerful Trade Union Group of Labour MPs.

A regular in the Tea Room was George Thomas who, though not a miner, had been brought up in the Rhondda Valley. A bachelor, he lived with his mother ('Mam' Thomas) whom he helped to make famous in her own right. She lived to a great age. George had trained as a teacher in Southampton and when he returned to the Rhondda 'plus fours' were in fashion. It was the early 1930s and the height of the industrial depression in South Wales. The miners, all out of work, tended to squat at the side of the road. As the newly qualified teacher walked down the street of Tonypandy in his 'plus fours', one miner quipped, 'George, are you working in water?' Despite achieving great eminence he always maintained close links with his native Rhondda. One day, he walked into one of the bars in the House of Commons and a

Tory came up to him and said, 'George, your tie, is it the Brigade of Guards?'

'No', was the reply, 'Tonypandy Co-op.'

One of his early ministerial appointments was that of Minister of State at the Commonwealth Office. As a Methodist lay-preacher one day he gave a sermon at a tribal gathering and then the local chieftain thanked him for bringing them the Christian message. 'It was wonderful,' he said, 'and though Mr Thomas is a white man, I am sure that inside his heart is as black as ours.'

Then there was S.O. Davies (Merthyr) who by this time must have turned eighty years of age. He wore a black coat and pinstriped trousers. A Baptist college-trained Minister, he was also a mining engineer and a former Vice-Chairman of the South Wales miners. Despite his age and advancing frailty he was a remarkable man, as he showed by standing as an Independent in the 1970 General Election and winning, when his own Constituency Party had thrown him out, alleging he was too old. Tudor Watkins, (Brecon and Radnor), was a wonderful election campaigner, as he clearly demonstrated by holding on to such a difficult seat for twenty-five years. Iorrie Thomas, (Rhondda West), was a remarkable character. An extremely able and shrewd man, he had been introduced to the Westminster scene at a rather late age. When asked what he was doing before he came to the Commons, he would reply, 'Waiting for Will John to die.' This was his predecessor, of course.

Roy Jenkins had won a by-election in London in the mid 1940s and shortly afterwards he was walking down the corridor near the tea room when Iorrie Thomas approached him and said, 'Congratulations – your father and I were in College together.' The famous son of Pontypool was rather taken aback and he replied, 'My father never went to College.'

'Oh, yes,' said Iorrie, 'Cardiff Jail.' From that day onwards,

Iorrie always maintained Roy Jenkins never spoke to him again. It must be said that their fathers were not in prison for any criminal activities but because of a miners' industrial dispute.

The Labour Government at this time were concerned about issues such as inflation and the Balance of Payments and they were keen to introduce an Incomes Policy. The Whips called upon a trade union worthy Iorrie Thomas to help out and support such a policy. There was much opposition to the Government's policy from Labour's ranks and a vociferous opponent was Eric Heffer (Liverpool Walton). In a speech Iorrie criticised Eric who in response shouted across the Chamber, 'I'll get you, mate.' The Member for Rhondda West coolly responded, 'I've lived near the woods too long to be frightened of owls.'

Arthur Pearson (Pontypridd) was a former Guardsman who at seventy was a tall and upright figure. A chainmaker by trade in his native Pontypridd, Arthur was a bachelor and it is said that throughout his thirty years in the House of Commons he never had a telephone in his home. For some years he was in the Whips' Office and from all accounts was a very tough Whip too. When Members enquired whether they could go home he invariably said, 'There might be another vote.' When Welsh MPs got on to the train at Paddington Station, however, they would often find Arthur already sitting in the carriage trying to hide his face behind a newspaper.

The doyen of the Welsh Labour Group was undoubtedly James Griffiths, the much respected Member for Llanelli. He had entered the House in 1936, having been President of the South Wales Miners' Federation. Welsh speaking, he was appointed by Clem Attlee in 1945 as Minister for National Insurance and during his years in that post he had helped to lay the basis for the Welfare State as we know it today. Despite being a septuagenarian, it was to him that Harold Wilson turned in 1964 to be the First Secretary of State for Wales. In later years I came to know his Private Secretary, who came from Newport. He told me that they had started the new Department with two pencils in a jam jar, so to speak. It was like Topsy though, for it just 'grew and grew'. Now it has been overtaken to some extent, following the creation of an elected Welsh Assembly.

The characters I met up with on the Welsh scene were not confined to South Wales. There were two brothers, Idwal and Tom Jones, who were Welsh speaking and came from the Rhos area. Idwal represented Wrexham; he was a scholar and former Headmaster, a very kind and friendly man. His brother Tom represented Merioneth. Self-taught, he was a Lay Preacher and Chairman of the local Magistrates' Bench.

Wrexham had a long tradition of lager drinking, with its own brewery in the town. Until recently, lager was practically unheard of in the pubs of South Wales. Cledwyn Hughes MP (Anglesey) used to tell us of the time he went with Tom to Llandrindod Wells in the Merioneth Constituency. It was a Sunday and those were the days when in Wales no pub was open on the Sabbath. They went, however, in to the Metropole Hotel and Cledwyn went up to the bar and said, 'What will you have, Tom?'

'A pint of lager,' he replied. Cledwyn handed him the pint glass whereupon some of Tom's constituents entered the bar. He promptly held up the pint of lager and said, 'Cledwyn, is this alcoholic?' There is more than a little hypocrisy in Wales about alcohol. Even now I tend to hide my glass if someone takes a photograph of me at a reception.

Tom and Idwal were travelling home by rail via Shrewsbury, when some youths threw stones at the train. Their carriage window was smashed and poor Idwal was cut by flying glass. Someone pulled the emergency cord and the train ground to a halt. It was realised that Idwal had been injured and quickly a steward came up with a glass of brandy for him. The Member for Wrexham, however, a genuine lifelong teetotaller, had a look of disdain on his face as he pushed the glass away. Sitting close to him was his brother Tom who said, 'I'll have it – I have had an awful shock.'

As I entered Parliament so Tom Jones retired but he was not lost to the Westminster scene and soon he was back as Lord Maelor. It was at this stage that the Merioneth Constituency Labour Party gave a dinner for their retiring MP and there were presentations to both him and his wife. Tom got up to respond and said, 'I want to thank you from the bottom of my heart and from my wife's bottom as well.' What a character! They don't come quite like that today.

Tom was not the best of letter writers and sometimes there was a delay in replying to correspondence. Cledwyn Hughes and, I think, Goronwy Roberts volunteered to go into the library to try and help him. There they found a pile of correspondence about two feet high. They tried to tackle this mass of letters but the task proved too formidable and they gave up.

One of the March 1966 intake was Elyston Morgan (Ceredigion 1966-74) and I became quite friendly with him. He was basically a Welsh Nationalist, a former member of Plaid Cymru and a Parliamentary candidate for that party. Eventually when James Callaghan became Home Secretary Elyston was appointed Under-Secretary at the Home Office. Unfortunately, he lost his seat in 1974.

Labour lost the election in 1970 but returned to power in 1974, when Harold Wilson appointed James Callaghan as Foreign Secretary. It is said that if Elyston had been around at the time Jim would have taken him to the Foreign Office. A year of two later Harold Wilson resigned and Callaghan became Prime Minister. Had Elyston been at the Foreign Office it is quite likely that he, rather than David Owen, would have become Foreign Secretary. Such an outcome would have avoided a few problems for Labour. Elyston was a fluent Welsh speaker but likewise he had a tremendous command of the English language with a kind of stained glass window oratory. At the time of entering the House he was a solicitor but subsequently became a barrister and later a circuit judge.

One of the difficulties for someone from the provinces on being elected to Parliament is that of accommodation. My predecessor Sir Frank Soskice strongly advised me to have my main home in London. In many ways this is sound advice, particularly if one is an out-and-out careerist. In London one could be near the action besides having the opportunity to socialise, which is one way, I suppose, of helping to climb the greasy pole.

In the event I took the advice of some Welsh colleagues and joined them in a boarding house near Paddington Station. My colleagues were Donald Coleman (Neath), Neil McBride (Swansea East), Cliff Williams (Abertillery), Elfed Davies (Rhondda East), Alec Jones (Rhondda West) and Ted Rowlands (Cardiff North). In those days the pay of Members of Parliament hardly provided for an expensive lifestyle. Some MPs of course had outside interests and other new entrants quickly made outside contacts and were able to supplement their income with consultancies of one kind or another. This mainly applied to Conservatives. Then there were the lawyers who seemed to be a law unto themselves on either side of the Party divide. They could 'pair off' so that their important legal work could be carried on without interruption.

There was a little enclave near Paddington Station where the boarding houses were owned by Welsh exiles. They were very friendly people and I suppose Welsh MPs helped to provide a useful income for them. Nevertheless, when the spring and summer arrived they were anxious to know how many nights we wished to book in for. Their trade tended to be seasonal and whereas in the winter months boarding houses were rather empty, as the year progressed the number of visitors increased. This caused difficulty because normally we would not know the business of the following week until the Thursday preceding it. To counteract this difficulty one of the devices we used was to catch the sleeper from Paddington to South Wales on a Thursday evening. We could board the train at about 10.30 p.m. but I recall it did not leave the station until about 12.50 a.m. and it took the long route around Gloucester. I would arrive in Newport at 5.20 a.m. and then I would pick up my car from the Kings Head Hotel which is near the station.

It was rather a miserable sort of existence. Cliff Williams (Abertillery) used to refer to the sleeper as the 'Old Shaker'. He detested it and it was probably one reason why he retired rather early from the House of Commons. This was not a very satisfactory way of organising our London life and in the early seventies when MPs' allowances were increased I decided to move into more permanent accommodation. This I found in Kilburn which is well known for its large Irish population. Indeed, it is known as the Irishtocracy. The flat I took was part of a substantial family house and the owners also ran an internationally famed hairdressing school in the West End. The flat overlooked the back garden and here I was most comfortable.

CHAPTER 8

Changes in Fortunes

Early in 1970 the mood in Labour ranks changed, as Kenneth Morgan, in his biography of Callaghan, says. 'It moved from bleak house to great expectations.' For three years we had been in the doldrums but now the polls were moving in favour of Labour. Quintin Hogg, the future Lord Chancellor, was horrified and I recall the unprintable language he used one evening near the ticker-tape in the Commons to express his concern at what was happening. There was at last a feeling that Labour could win the General Election. The man most identified with Labour's changed fortunes was the Chancellor Roy Jenkins. The hard slog following devaluation now seemed to be paying off and evidence of this came in trade surpluses over several months. A solid Balance of Payments surplus was revealed and likewise the gold and foreign exchange reserves went up.

In electoral terms the change in Labour's fortunes was clearly shown in the South Ayrshire by-election on 19 March 1970, when Jim Sillers won a splendid victory. Hitherto, throughout the life of the Parliament Labour had found it well-nigh impossible to win a by-election in Scotland. The contest was brought about on account of the death of Emrys Hughes who originally came from Pontypridd. He had earlier gone up to Scotland to edit the Socialist journal *Forward* and while based there had married Keir Hardie's daughter. A popular character, he was something of a maverick and at one stage had the Whip withdrawn for voting against the defence estimates.

I found Jim Sillers a very bright and pleasant character, with a solid working class background. He had been a local official of the Fire Brigades Union and subsequently had worked for the Scottish TUC. Personally I believe he was a 'natural' to become Secretary of State for Scotland in the years ahead but he soon became disillusioned with the policies of the Labour Government. It has also been suggested that there was keen rivalry between him and Neil Kinnock that led to some bitterness. He resigned the Labour Whip in July 1976 and thereafter sat as a member of the Scottish Labour Party of which he was a founder, but he lost his seat to the official Labour candidate in the General Election of 1979.

Unfortunately the budget of 14 April was not popular enough to win over the electors. Likewise, after a June election had been decided upon, Harold Wilson did not project a forward-looking socialist vision which might have helped at the polls. In Newport we canvassed vigorously. One of my most hard-working supporters was Alf Lovell, who had been Mayor of Newport and the Returning Officer when I was first elected four years earlier. He had spent a lifetime at Lysaghts steelworks and was a great loyalist. I recall him stomping around the estates with a huge megaphone, proclaiming our message. We had a good campaign and felt optimistic about the outcome. The night before the eve of the poll, Harold Wilson, as Prime Minister, made the customary pre-election broadcast. I was in the Gunners Club down Pill★ and Harold appeared like the cat who had whipped the cream. I thought we were home and dry, as did we all. Political journalists travelled around the country and to various meetings and press conferences. They became convinced that a Labour victory was inevitable and the opinion polls told a similar story. In the event there was a uniform swing to the Conservatives

---

★ A local expression, short for Pwllgwenlly, the cradle of Newport, close to the docks.

throughout the country. The poll was down from 75.8 per cent in 1966 to 72 per cent. When the result became clear the Conservatives had won 350 seats, Labour 288, Liberals six and the Scottish Nationalists one (Western Isles). In Newport the polls showed a swing of 0.1 per cent to the Conservatives. The result was 30,132 Labour, 22,005 Conservatives and 1,997 Plaid Cymru, a Labour majority of 8,127. In Wales we lost Cardiff North, Monmouth, Pembroke and Conway but at least Carmarthen was won back from the Nationalists. There was a sensational victory in Merthyr, where the veteran S.O. Davies, who had stood as an unofficial Labour candidate, defeated the official Transport House endorsed candidate.

Many issues had played their part in Labour's defeat. The war in Vietnam for one thing had deterred young people and political idealists. The bruising encounter within the Party and with the Trade Unions over 'In Place of Strife' had also taken its toll. There was not the clamour of activists to move out of Labour strongholds to campaign in marginal seats. My own majority was slightly down. Overall the result was very disappointing. On polling night Marion and I had booked into the historic Westgate Hotel but we left early the following morning, too dejected to have breakfast, even a full English one.

The 1970 General Election seemed to be quite a watershed in the history of the Labour Party and this was particularly so in Wales. It marked the retirement of so many longstanding Members such as James Griffiths (Llanelli), Harold Finch (Bedwellty), Arthur Pearson (Pontypridd), Eirene White (West Flint) and Tudor Watkins (Brecon and Radnor). They were replaced by Denzil Davies, Neil Kinnock, Brynmor John, Barry Jones and Caerwyn Roderick. Donald Anderson was defeated in Monmouth and Ted Rowlands in Cardiff but both were to return fairly quickly to the House in comparatively safe seats. What soon became apparent was that all the new intake were ambitious. It was not for them to sit at the Welsh table in the tea room to reminisce about days that were gone

The House of Commons and the House of Lords are both housed in the Palace of Westminster which was once a royal residence. It has been adapted over the years to meet the needs of Parliament but it is hardly purpose-built. There was a clamour for offices and desks which had hitherto been in short supply. Many Members tended to work in the library where there was an adequate supply of stationery. I recall standardised printed forms to take up an issue with a Minister; there was another to acknowledge the complaint of one's constituent and a further one to be sent out with the Minister's reply. Such routine procedures did not require a very high degree of literary skill. Soon secretarial allowances were introduced and these have gradually been increased over the years. In addition, research assistants became the vogue and are now employed by almost every Member. Evidence of this development can easily be seen by a visit to the Members' cafeteria at lunch time. There can he found hordes of Members' staff. It looks like a works canteen – the food is excellent.

One who did not accept the changes was the Rt. Hon. Enoch Powell who throughout his Parliamentary career continued to work in the library, writing out his speeches with an ink pen.

In the 1970-74 Parliament the major issue, apart from Europe, was Industrial Relations. After the debacle over 'In Place of Strife', the new Conservative Prime Minister Ted Heath was determined to bring in a Tory version of this infamous document. The Queen's Speech in July revealed that a 'Bill will be introduced to establish a framework of law within which improved industrial relations can develop and a code of practice will be prepared laying down standards for good management and trade union practices'. This Bill had a very stormy passage through the House of Commons. There was one demonstration in the Chamber involving the mace, in which Tribune group members like Stan Orme, Eric Heffer and Ian Mikardo used obstructive tactics. The Speaker (Selwyn Lloyd) suspended the sitting but when proceedings resumed he chose to ignore the protestors rather than make martyrs of them. Perhaps the most colourful demonstration against the Bill took place in the early hours of the morning of 28 January 1971. There was a guillotine motion to curtail discussion and in the event the Commons voted continuously from midnight until 4.45 a.m. A total of twenty-four divisions took place without a single word of debate. In the final vote in the Division Lobby, Welsh Members began to sing 'The Red Flag'. It was taken up on all sides and continued not only in the voting lobby but also in the Chamber itself. I was rather fascinated to see some of the most reactionary elements in Labour's ranks singing lustily what at least until recently has been acknowledged as our Party's anthem. The Tories seemed to be rather dumbfounded. Some made a quick exit, others jeered and a handful took coins from their pocket and flicked them across the Chamber. Eventually the House adjourned at 5.27 a.m. Events such as this tend to remain in one's memory.

On 30 January 1971 *The Times* had a three column leading article headed 'Dangers of the Glee Club'. It spoke of extraordinary scenes in the House of Commons . . . 'which are bound to offend public opinion'. It concluded 'Labour will never convince the electorate that they would provide a better Government unless the leadership demonstrates in the days of Opposition that it is in control of the Party.'

The Bill became law but that was far from the end of the story because it became virtually unenforceable. Five dockers were sent to prison for picketing the Midland Cold Storage Company but on 1 August 1972 the 'Pentonville Five', as they became known, were released on the authority of the House of Lords without having purged their contempt.

James Callaghan, who by now had replaced Barbara Castle as employment spokesman, said at the time, 'Industrial relations could not be run by barristers' courts, writs of contempt and the full panoply of the law.'

Things came to a head in January and February 1972 with the first national strike by the miners since 1926. It was brought about due to the fact that the miners had fallen behind in the wage league table. Arthur Scargill's secondary picketing at Saltby coke depot raised a few eyebrows, not least amongst the Labour leadership. In the event the Wilberforce Court of Inquiry recommended an increase of some twenty-two per cent. The Government and the CBI were anxious to settle because a good deal of disruption was being caused to industry but there was still reluctance on the part of the miners.

On 18 February Ted Heath invited the miners' leaders to Number Ten Downing Street for talks which went on until the early hours of the morning. Joe Gormley the Miners' President was, it appears, ready to settle but his two lieutenants, Mick McGahey and Arthur Scargill, were more intransigent. Eventually but grudgingly the miners' leaders gave up their demand for more pay and settled for concessions on fringe benefits.

After the defeat in the 1970 General Election turbulent times followed for the Labour Party. It was a period of considerable unrest, with an increasing division between right and left. The Parliamentary Party symbolised the right, whereas the left concentrated on the constituencies. Militants as well came to the fore in the trade unions, rejecting any wage restraint and urging more nationalisation and central controls over the economy. At this time a new charismatic leader emerged in the person of Anthony Wedgwood Benn who changed his name to Tony Benn. He had come to believe that Labour had lost because they pursued negative right-wing policies which had disillusioned their supporters. This assertion contrasted with his earlier position as a centrist and technocratic member of the Wilson Government, pro-Europe, pro-NATO and a supporter of Barbara Castle's Industrial Relations Bill. Likewise, he now called for a fundamental reappraisal of Labour's economic and international policies, together with a call for a revamping of the constitution of the Party to give grass roots supporters and militants far more influence on the leadership and policy making procedures. It was a conversion of Damascene proportions and many have since called into question Benn's political judgment.

Labour's internal divisions, however, were balanced out by the endless crises of the Heath Government which reached their climax with the trauma of another national miners' strike which reduced Britain to a three-day working week. Heath was eventually persuaded to call a General Election on 18 February 1974, based on the slogan of 'Who Governs Britain'.

Labour supporters were not very optimistic about the outcome and as I went around our Labour Clubs the opinion seemed to be that, whereas I would win in Newport, we were not likely to get a Labour Government. To make matters worse, I recall polling night in Newport when around six o'clock, normally the most popular time for voting, it was as black as night and raining heavily. Marion as always was with me but just a little bit distressed as she said, 'I'll be glad when tonight is over.'

In the campaign Labour spokesmen had emphasised their ability to avoid industrial conflict and as James Callaghan pointed out, 'Fixing wages by law means tension, unfairness and strikes.'

There was a poll of 78.8 per cent, six points up on 1970, and the highest turnout since 1951. Labour, however, with only slight gains, won 301 seats, compared with the Conservatives 297. What proved decisive was the strong showing of the Liberals who, although winning fourteen seats, nevertheless increased their poll share from 7.5 per cent in 1970 to 19.3 per cent with over 6 million votes.

In Newport we had a splendid victory. Compared with 1970 the turnout went up from 71,520 to 75,412 and I had a majority of 11,382. The polling figures were as follows:

R.J. Hughes (Labour)	29,384
G. Price (Con)	18,002
J.H. Morgan (Liberal)	11,868
Mrs P. Cox (Plaid)	936

Heath★ proposed a coalition with the Liberals and Jeremy Thorpe indicated that his Party was much closer to the Conservatives than to Labour on the major issues of the day, such as Europe and a Prices & Incomes policy. Thorpe was anxious to become Home Secretary but before the meeting with the Prime Minister took place, the Secretary of the Cabinet warned Heath that there were matters in Thorpe's private life, as yet undisclosed to the public, which might make this a highly unsuitable position for him to hold. Thorpe was eventually forced to forget any link-up with the Tories, following representations from supporters all over the country who were very much opposed to such a link-up.

Meanwhile, Labour's strategy was to leave Heath dangling until eventually he was forced to announce his inability to form a Government and he resigned. Harold Wilson became Prime Minister for a third time but he was weary and his health was not good. James Callaghan became Foreign Secretary and his principal task seems to have been to oversee the renegotiation of our entry terms to the Common Market. In the event this amounted to much ado about nothing. He seemed to have sold out on the central question of British sovereignty and appeared to think that the industrial and

---

★Ted Heath 'The Course of my Life' (p.518).

regional policy aspects were not worth emphasising as major points for renegotiation.

At the time Peter Shore and Tony Benn were critical of Callaghan's stance, in the back of whose mind might have been a feeling that the unknown might of Brussels could perhaps be wheeled in to help frustrate what he regarded as the wider excesses of Benn's 'alternative economic strategy with its massive directive powers over British industry'.★

Wilson eventually called a second election for 10 October and went to the country on a relatively moderate manifesto. It was quite an uninspiring affair and the result was disappointing for Wilson and his colleagues. Labour's total of 319 seats meant an overall majority of only three with a swing of just one per cent in its favour. My result, though, was again very pleasing and there was an even higher poll, up from 74.55 per cent in February 1974 to 75.4 per cent.

Roy Hughes (Lab)	30,069
G. Price (Cons)	16,253
J.H. Morgan (Lib)	9,207
G. Lea (Plaid)	2,216
	13,816 majority

My agent in Newport for both 1974 General Elections was Graham Wilson. He was originally from the north of England and besides having a First Class degree he was a splendid colleague in every way. His wife Ingrid is a charming person. Graham and I worked very closely together throughout both campaigns and the results were rewarding. One amusing incident I recall was a visit to a Workingmen's Club off the Chepstow Road. In the bar was a nude portrait decorating the wall and in order to restore at least a modicum of decency to the young lady we posted a 'Vote for Roy Hughes' sticker on a pivotal part of her body.

★*Callaghan, A Life* – Ken O'Morgan.

CHAPTER 9

The Common Market

ONE POLICY ISSUE that dominated the 1970-74 Parliament was our entry into Europe, or the Common Market as it was known then. It was a fateful decision and I have always believed it to be the biggest mistake made by our country since the end of the Second World War.

Ted Heath and his Government had no mandate to take us in but any such moral impediment was ruthlessly swept aside. When the vote took place on the principle of entry, fifty-nine Labour MPs voted with the Heath Government and twenty more abstained. If all Labour had voted against, and in line with our Party's policy, then, together with the support of some Tory defectors, the measure could have been defeated. It is worth pointing out too that numerous Labour MPs who voted with the Heath Government later defected when the attempt was made to form the Social Democratic Party. Names like David Owen and David Marquand come to mind. This latter action did tremendous harm to the fortunes of the Labour Party and laid the basis for the long period of Thatcherism. I witnessed the active co-operation of certain Labour MPs (even senior ones) with Tory whips. The tactic seemed to be that when the Government was certain of winning a division then they would vote with their own Party, but if there was a possibility of a Government defeat then they would stay out of the voting lobby.

There was one division when Labour's Whips office felt there was a chance of winning and presumably the leadership had to give the impression that they were actually opposing this Tory measure. By now I was heartily sick of the whole business and I had arranged to pair with Harmer Nicholls (later Lord), the Member for Peterborough, who was very much a Euro sceptic. As I recall we were coming up to the Whitsun recess so I started to make my way to Paddington Station by way of the underground. When I got to the taxi rank at the Members' entrance, the policeman there said to me, 'Mr Hughes, Mr Walter Harrison (Labour's Deputy Chief Whip) wishes to speak to you.' I ignored this request but when I was sitting in the train at Paddington Station, waiting to depart for South Wales, a message came over the tannoy. 'Will Mr Roy Hughes please return to Westminster.' Needless to say I ignored this request as well! I am afraid that when I dig my heels in I can be pretty resolute. As a boy in Nine Mile Point Colliery I recall being told, 'You gotta be solid see, butt' and this little exhortation has always stayed in my mind.

Personally I spoke many times in opposition to our joining and later in the call for us to withdraw. Nevertheless, the multinationals were in favour and they tended to cross the boundaries of nation states as if they were of little more consequence than County Council boundaries. One American-owned multinational company with a factory in Newport went so far as to put a note in the pay packet of each worker indicating that if there was a 'No' vote then the company would relocate on the continent. This was the kind of blackmail that was being used at the time. Likewise the British media were very strongly in favour of our joining. What has irritated me in particular is the deceitful way the Pro-Europeans have gone about the task of fulfilling the objectives set out in the Treaty of Rome. They have shown a determination to establish, by whatever means, the foundations of an ever closer union among the European peoples. Campaigning, though, has almost always been on the economic benefits of union. In Britain integration has always been played down but the speeches and declarations coming from Europe cover currency and monetary policy, trade, defence, police, justice and much else. These moves are designed to bring closer a United States of Europe. To this day the European Union is still portrayed as being primarily about economic matters and the British people are being deceived as never before.

EU leaders have stated that monetary union is the motor of European integration. 'A European army and a European police force lie at the end of the road to European Union' (Jean-Luc Dehaene, Prime Minister of Belgium). Helmut Kohl, the former German Chancellor has also stated his belief that the objective of the Council of Ministers is to secure far more power over the budgets of member states.

As an experienced politician having spent over thirty-five years in Westminster, I am quite sure that these are not the desired objectives of the British people. They have been led by the nose and public opinion polls over the years have repeatedly borne out this analysis.

At the time of the 1997 General Election in Britain, Tony Blair, the Leader of the Labour Party, in a major policy article in the *Sun* newspaper, said, 'New Labour will have no truck with a European superstate. We will fight for British interests and to keep our independence very inch of the way.' With great respect to our Prime Minister, all I can say is that the reality has been a little bit different.

The Nice Treaty increases the powers of the EU, *vis-à-vis* member states, on defence, taxation, policing border controls, industrial and trade policy, the virtual abolition of the veto, and even control over what kind of political parties will be allowed to exist. We are repeatedly being told by Government Ministers that if we were to join the Euro currency it would have no constitutional significance. I am reminded of the story of the Duke of Wellington walking on London Bridge when a man came up to him and said, 'Mr John Smith, I believe.' The

Duke turned to him and said, 'Sir, if you believe that, you will believe anything.'

The British people should have the right to be told the truth and then they can make up their minds what they want done with their currency, their laws and legal traditions, their police, their armed forces, their democracy and their capacity to govern themselves. This is what democracy is all about. It is interesting to note what happened in Denmark in their referendum on the Euro held on 28 September 2000. A small, modern, democratic country rejected the Euro by fifty-three per cent in an almost ninety per cent poll. Yet without exception the political establishment, the media and the business community all advocated joining. How out of touch can you get and on such an important issue? I venture to suggest that the feelings of the British people are not altogether different from those of the Danish people.

In the early days of the Heath Government when the European legislation was being put through Parliament Labour MPs were on a three-line whip to oppose it. Unfortunately what we witnessed was little short of treachery on the part of sixty-nine Jenkinsite rebels, for they voted with the Tory Government and thus ensured that the legislation went through. Had we stuck together we could have won and defeated the entry proposals for there was also a handful of Tories who were opposed to it and voted accordingly. It was Labour Europhile MPs who ensured a continued Parliamentary majority for Heath and even supported him when the Government guillotined the debate. The Treaty which these rebels supported undermined the supremacy of Parliament and the ultimate authority of the British courts.

As a country we had to abandon our long developed low-cost food supplies from Canada, Australia and New Zealand. Instead, we had to embrace the high cost Common Agricultural Policy and help absorb the surpluses of French farmers.

Imperial preference – tariff-free access to the UK market of Commonwealth manufactured goods – also had to be abandoned. In fact an external tariff was imposed by the Common Market on these goods. A new system of indirect taxation (VAT) was introduced and our own purchase tax on luxury and semi-luxury items, with total purchase tax exemption on all necessities, such as food and clothing, had to be abandoned. The UK had to accept the Community's new system of self-taxation to finance the common policies of which the French-designed Common Agricultural Policy was the most expensive. What a travesty the whole exercise has been and what a surrender for a country that played such a major part in the outcome of the Second World War!

Some time later George Thomas (Viscount Tonypandy) said to me in a very friendly way, 'Forget it now, Roy, it is all over'. This I have found is the normal way with major political issues once they have been settled. However strong the arguments might have been, normally the outcome is accepted. Personally on this European issue I have never been able to accept the outcome and it is becoming ever more apparent that it is an ongoing issue. What I found rather ironic was that George Thomas, despite his advice to me years ago, on his death bed was bitterly opposing the European Union, particularly over the issue of British sovereignty. The British people as a whole, I feel, are as agnostic as ever for they will not accept this concept of our country being a part of an ever deeper European Union. A major criticism of Europe is the sheer waste of resources. For example fraud runs into billions of pounds and despite all the exhortations over the years little seems to have been done about it.

The Assembly, or the so-called European Parliament, has minimal power to control the European Commission but the cost is prohibitive. A Parliamentary Question was put down by Lord Tenby on 5 July 2000 to try and ascertain the true cost.

He asked 'What is the annual cost of maintaining the European Parliament, the House of Commons and the House of Lords, including:-

    (a) salaries, pensions, travelling allowances, secretarial expenses and other expenses for Members.

    (b) salaries, allowances and pensions and other costs of support staff.

    (c) accommodation, including rent, operating costs and security, and

    (d) all other administrative costs such as stationery, office equipment, publications, payments to parliamentary bodies and other relevant outgoings;

and whether they will indicate the per capita cost per Member as well as the average number of sitting days for each institution for 1999-2000 and the previous four years.'

Lord McIntosh of Haringey divulged the information for 1999-2000 as follows:

Total Costs 1999-2000	£ million
House of Lords	45.3
House of Commons	263.7
European Parliament	610
of which cost to UK is	102.7

Per capita cost per member 1999-2000	£'000
House of Lords	37
House of Commons	400
European Parliament	974

Number of sitting days 1999-2000	
House of Lords	158
House of Commons	157
European Parliament	60

In 1975 came the Referendum which had been promised by Harold Wilson, partly in his effort to hold the Labour Party together despite its divisions over Europe. The Cabinet decided by sixteen votes to seven to stay in the EEC and from then on the dice was loaded heavily in favour of a 'Yes' vote. Three documents were to be issued, the first putting the arguments in favour of staying in, the second putting the case for withdrawing and the third putting the Government's point of view, i.e. to remain a member.

With the exception of the Communist *Daily Worker* (*Morning Star*) every newspaper made the call for a 'yes' vote. Radio and TV were little different. There had earlier been a rather interesting development within the Parliamentary Labour Party with the decision, prompted by the Pro-Europeans, to form a Europe Group. Some of us who were 'Anti' went along to the first meeting, which we were perfectly entitled to do. In the event John Mendelson (MP Sheffield Penistone) nominated me for the Chair and I was elected. The 'Pros', it seemed, had not attended the Committee (their brainchild) in sufficient numbers. Subsequently I was invited to speak in various parts of the country including Coventry, Taunton, Dover and a Synagogue in the East End of London. The meeting in Coventry I particularly enjoyed because my opponent was Alick Dick who had been Managing Director of the Standard Motor Company when I first went to work there. He was ousted from his position when Leyland took over. We spoke in the precincts of the new Cathedral and I must say that by then my enthusiasm and Welsh *hwyl* were coming to the forefront. By contrast my opponent more or less apologised for his speaking performance and said 'These MPs . . .'

Another visit I made about this time was to Milan and I was accompanied by John Mendelson and by Raymond Fletcher (MP for Ilkeston). The object of the visit was to meet up with the Italian Left to get an idea of their attitude to membership of the Common Market. When we sat down for the cross table discussions both of my colleagues asked that I should take the lead and open the discussions. For a moment I was somewhat taken aback because John Mendelson and Ray Fletcher were both very experienced lecturers, but fortunately I had become well conversant with the subject.

My jaw dropped when at the end of my remarks Roy Fletcher said it was the best layman's exposition of the case against Britain's membership of the Common Market that he had heard. Our Italian friends were much more partial to membership and I formed the opinion that they were putting forward a rather Trotskyist point of view, based on the idea of uniting the workers of Europe.

This Italian visit was most worthwhile and it was capped by a visit to La Scala on the Sunday evening. I would have liked to see an opera performed there but in the event we had to make do with a programme of classical music. In the foyer there were characters rather like Beefeaters and I was interested and impressed to see a statue of the composer Giuseppe Verdi whom I always associate with 'The March of the Hebrew Slaves' from *Nabucco* (1842). This is one of my favourite pieces of music and when sung by a Welsh Male Voice Choir I find it quite inspirational. It was, of course, the theme song of Garibaldi and his followers in their campaign for the unification of Italy.

While the Referendum campaign was going on, Sir Donald Stokes (later to become Lord Stokes) was putting full-page advertisements in our leading daily newspapers, pointing out how essential it was to get a 'Yes' vote because then he would be able to sell many thousands of motor cars on the continent. In the event these pretensions proved to be quite mythical and the number of cars sold to our European partners was derisory to say the least.

The Referendum was held in June 1975 and produced a large majority of votes to stay in the Community. Going around the doors in the campaign I found a lack of understanding of what the vote was about. My constituents asked 'If we come out who are we going to trade with?' They seem to have believed that Volkswagen, Mercedes, Renault and Fiat were going to refuse to sell us their motor cars and I was saddened to see how the pro-Europe campaign had misled people. Working class people are understandably apprehensive about the possibility of being put out of work and I believe this factor played a major part in bringing about a 'Yes' vote. In reality the twenty-five years that followed our joining the Common Market was hardly a period of prosperity for Britain. Unemployment rose not once but twice to record over three million. Major sectors of British industry were simply wiped out. Being a member of the Community certainly did not bring prosperity to our country for by 1979 the bubble had burst. Our financial contributions to Europe are prohibitive and in the period since we joined in 1973 our net payment has amounted to the staggering total of £40 billion. The annual contribution is now running at roughly two to three billion pounds a year. It is worth considering what benefits such amounts could bring to our health and education services.

Now the pressure is on for Britain to join the Euro and we are assured by members of the Government that this will have no major constitutional significance. Again the emphasis is on narrow economic issues but I would have thought that for any country to forsake its currency puts it very much on a slippery slope. It is obviously a major part of the process of European integration with the eventual objective of a Super State.

On Monday 9 April 2001 there was a very important legal ruling in a court in Sunderland to the effect that it is a criminal offence to sell a pound of bananas. Yet opinion polls have shown that over ninety per cent of the British people are opposed to using the criminal law to enforce exclusive use of the metric system in this country. Mr Justice Morgan was brutally clear in pointing out that there is no way the British people, let alone a British court, any longer have the right to argue on this point. Thirty years ago, he said, we voluntarily decided as a nation to join the European Union. Our politicians voluntarily decided on our behalf to accept that exclusive use of the metric system should be made compulsory in this country by Brussels directives and also that a British court cannot rule as illegal any law approved in Brussels. Our Parliament has accepted that the European Union has supreme sovereignty.

Mr Thoburn, the stall holder who had been prosecuted, was not forcing his customers to buy fruit in pounds and ounces for he also had a set of metric scales. If a customer asked for half a kilo of bananas that is what would be given but the vast majority of his customers preferred to buy in pounds and ounces. This legal ruling obviously has deep implications for the way this country is now governed and I hope and trust it helps to alert the British people to what is happening. I am crystal clear in my own mind that the last thing the British people want is a United States of Europe with Britain relegated to regional status, an off-shore island. By contrast there is every evidence that British citizens want close and friendly relations with their continental neighbours. They want to be able to travel freely in Europe and most believe in free trade throughout the continent. Increasing numbers of people from Britain have been able to experience for themselves the diversity and variety of European cultural, sporting and entertainment events and have thoroughly enjoyed doing so. There is no lack of friendship and goodwill. This is very different, however, from giving up our own legal and democratic traditions that are so different from those on the continent.

Understandably people may well ask why am I so anti-Europe and it is not an easy question to answer. What I can say is that I am not a little Englander, or whatever its Welsh equivalent might be, although I have a great love for the Land of my Fathers. I have always taken a keen interest in international affairs and immediately I entered the House of Commons I joined both the Inter-Parliamentary Union and the Commonwealth Parliamentary Association. These are the two bodies which link our Parliament with legislatures throughout the world. At one stage I was Treasurer of the IPU but was later forced to withdraw on account of an eye complaint which could have resulted in the loss of my sight.

CHAPTER 10

Parliamentary Delegations, Conferences and The Council of Europe

I BECAME AN OFFICER of many Parliamentary groups, including Bulgaria, Rumania and Hungary. Together with Don Dixon (Jarrow)* and Ray Powell (Ogmore)† who later became Senior Whips, I took part in a delegation to Rumania. We found it a frightful place and this of course was in the days of Ceausescu. We were installed in a Government hospitality villa which was well cordoned off and guarded. We had a male waiter to attend to our needs. My colleague Ray Powell had brought along a packet of tea bags which he handed over to the waiter. He left us and duly returned with a large brown enamel teapot. To our amazement and amusement we discovered that he had used the whole packet of tea bags for one pot of tea. He obviously believed in a strong brew!

The state-owned shops were bereft of any quality consumer goods and packs of 200 Marlboro cigarettes took precedence over the official currency. We were closely supervised throughout the visit. Perhaps the climax for me was a visit to a large factory producing TVs and radios. Hundreds of people were employed here and I recall that the ceilings were very low. We were chaperoned by a group of Communist officials and the black looks on the faces of the workers is something I shall never forget. Another incident which left its mark on me during this visit was when we visited a College of Further Education. It was in a pleasant part of the country with a lovely

---

*Lord Dixon of Jarrow.
†Sir Ray Powell.

125

sunny climate. There were hordes of students in the campus
and there was a walkway leading to the entrance of the College.
We arrived in a small convoy of black official cars and, as the
students were milling around towards the entrance, these cars
sped up through the middle of the crowd. One student was hit,
perhaps only a glancing blow but I thought that this was a
dreadful way to treat people.

This situation reminded me of going to see Newport
County when they were in the Football League. There was a
lane at the side of Somerton Park, where spectators walked to
the turnstiles of the ground. In my car I used to proceed up
this lane inches at a time for fear of hitting someone. There
seemed to be no such inhibitions in this alleged 'Socialist'
paradise of Rumania.

Earlier I had twice visited Eastern Germany (GDR) and
went to see the Leipzig Fair. At that time the GDR was not
recognised by our Government and therefore there could be
no official reciprocal hospitality. As a result some of us made a
contribution to enable a group of their Parliamentarians to visit
this country.

Several times I attended the World Peace Council which
tended to be under the wing of the Soviet Union. Nevertheless, I felt it did some good in bringing people together
from different parts of the globe in pursuit of world peace. In
saying this, I have never been a member of the Communist
Party nor any Trotskyist organisation. In Coventry I was
consistently invited to join one or the other but I have always
maintained a sort of critical loyalty to the Labour Party which I
joined as a youngster. I have, I suppose, been essentially
motivated by Aneurin Bevan. We came from the same valley
(Sirhowy); he came from the top (Tredegar) while I came from
lower down (Pontllanfraith) where the valley broadens. It is a
coincidence too that we both served for thirty-one years in the
House of Commons.

After one of the World Peace Conferences I was deputed, together with Sean MacBride the former Irish Prime Minister, to take a resolution on the Middle East to the United Nations Headquarters in New York. My Irish colleague had an illustrious background, having been awarded both the Nobel Peace Prize and the Star of Lenin but we got on famously. He was very down-to-earth. Our task was to deposit the resolution which called upon Israel to withdraw from occupied territories, and then to meet the international press. I am glad to say it all went very smoothly.

Soon after I entered the House of Commons I quickly became aware of the injustice that had been done to the Palestinians. In June 1967 there was war in the Middle East and I sat rather bemused in the Chamber listening to the points of view being expressed. When I heard calls from Sir Barnett Janner* about the 'Dunkirk spirit' and comparing the conflict with the Battle of Britain, I began to sit up and take notice. My knowledge of the Middle East was limited but at least I had seen a bit of war. My curiosity was aroused regarding the rights and wrongs of the conflict and I developed a thirst to find out more. I read a number of books on the subject and began to take an interest in some Arab groups. A colleague, David Watkins (MP Consett), seemed to have had a similar reaction to mine. We formed the Labour Middle East Council with Christopher Mayhew, a former Foreign Office Minister, who became Chairman, while I became Vice-Chairman and David Watkins the Treasurer.

In the Parliamentary Labour Party there was rather a starry-eyed view of Israel and anyone who questioned this viewpoint was quickly trampled upon and described as anti-Semitic. Golda Meir, the Israeli Prime Minister, had said there were no such people as Palestinians yet, at the time, several million of

*Later Lord Janner.

them were in refugee camps exiled from their homeland. I thought the newly-formed Labour Middle East Council brought a sense of realism to the situation in the Middle East and gradually the Labour Party in Parliament and the country as a whole tended to support this view. I became an officer of several Middle East groups including Egypt, Syria and Lebanon and over the years as a result of my interest and activities I was able to travel extensively in this troubled part of the world.

In 1982 I 'hit the headlines' in our local newspaper the *South Wales Argus*. At the time I was taking part in a delegation to Palestine which had been organised by the UK Palestinian Parliamentary Group. One day in a convoy we were in the Israeli-occupied West Bank. Suddenly a group of young men with masked faces threw stones at our vehicles, shouting out 'Al Fatah!'

'Hell's bells,' I muttered to myself – 'I'm on your side.' Instantly an Israeli in an approaching vehicle jumped out and started firing at the youths. We ducked rapidly and one of the delegation, Tom Benyon MP (Abingdon), said afterwards that the bullets missed us by inches. The heading in the *Argus* was 'Gwent MP escapes in shooting incident.'

An Inter-Parliamentary Union Conference is held every six months in various parts of the world. In 1990 we went to Uruguay. On the conclusion of the Conference I was able to realise a long-held ambition to visit Patagonia. It was a wonderful experience. We were accompanied by my Parliamentary colleague, Tom Cox (Tooting), a Londoner who had been evacuated to Oakdale near my home and brought up by his aunt. He became an electrician in the North Celynen pit.

Our visit coincided with the 125th anniversary of the arrival of 153 Welsh people on the Patagonian coast in search of a new home. The project had been carefully put in place by co-

With Tom Cox, MP, in Patagonia.

operation with the Argentinian Government who were anxious to attract 'hard-working immigrants from Northern Europe'. On the other side of the coin the Welsh travellers wished to escape from the relentless pressure on their way of life. All they wanted was to be left in peace to preserve their culture which had been sadly eroded by industrialisation. Their native language was being heartlessly wiped out and pressure was on them to abandon their Free Church culture.

They were to be the first group to arrive, the object being to attract between 300 and 500 immigrants each year for the next ten years. In the event by the year 1876 more than 500 had sailed from Wales and a further twenty-seven from New York. Most of the immigrants were young couples with children. By 1915 the population of the Chubut Valley, where they settled, had reached 12,000 of whom just over 4,000 were of Welsh descent.

The deal worked out with the Government looked attractive – a generous allotment of land tax free and the promise of republic status when the population reached 20,000. It seems that the agreement was a kind of enlightened self-interest on the part of the Argentine Government, for they were anxious to consolidate their position in Patagonia to which Chile laid claim. And, too, the Government wished for the native Indians, mostly nomads of the Tehuelche tribe, and the Welsh immigrants to live together harmoniously in order to put the whole area on a firm basis. On the whole they got on well together (apart from the time when the Indians demanded alcohol as part of their trading arrangements – this caused some knotted eyebrows on the part of the abstemious Welsh).

And so it was in 1865 that the Welsh contingent sailed on the *Mimosa*, a cargo vessel, having paid twelve pounds for the fare (children half-price) – an enormous sum in those days. The land where they settled in the Chubut Valley seems to have been full of contrasts. There was both fertile land and 'bad land'; floods and droughts. Darwin said of it when he visited the area, 'The Plains of Patagonia are covered with thorny bushes and a dry looking grass. It will forever remain nearly useless to mankind, for the curse of sterility is upon the land', but the Welsh people worked hard on the land to cultivate it and make the enterprise viable. Over the years they introduced irrigation schemes – real pick and shovel work. They were delighted with the climate and found it most health-giving. Here they were able to establish their own way of life and preserve their language without being persecuted by the English. Their life was most orderly. The focal point in the village was of course the Chapel which was also used as a Court and a grain depot. Indeed worshippers used sacks of grain as pews. All events of public interest were held in the chapel. In all thirty-one Chapels and three Churches were built in the valley.

On arriving in Trelew, the chief town in the area with a population of 100,000, we were warmly welcomed by our Welsh hosts and our visit was truly memorable. One of our hosts was a teacher called Eluned Gonzalez, who had previously been the principal guest on Visitors' Day at the National Eisteddfod of Wales, when speakers of the Gaelic language are especially welcomed.

In Trelew there is an impressive public hall called after Wales' patron Saint, Dewi Sant, and it was here we were invited to a large tea party. We recall the vast number of Welsh cakes in circulation. After tea I was asked to make a speech which I gladly did. It was then translated into both Welsh and Spanish. We were taken up the Chubut Valley to see the Welsh chapels. There was an overwhelming sense of emptiness wherever we went that day. It is a huge area stretching westwards to the foothills of the Andes. The chapels, which are carefully preserved, are austere in the extreme. A formidable bible had been placed on the lectern and that was all. It was interesting to see the names on the tombstones – Jones, Davies, Williams, Hughes etc – just like a Welsh village. The journey up the Chubut Valley was indeed a pilgrimage.

Before our journey to South America, Marion had mentioned to one of her colleagues on the Magistrates' Bench, Eirwen Thomas, that we were going to Patagonia. Eirwen asked if we could trace one of her relatives, an uncle called Hutchings, who had emigrated there. In this connection one day we were entertained by the young Mr Williams who was Mayor (Intendente) of a village called Dolafon.* We asked him if he knew of anyone called Hutchings and he said, 'Yes, he was my great-grandfather.' Apparently he had emigrated when a

---

*meaning River Meadows.

railway line was being built and after the work was completed
he was given some land to cultivate.

In these days of long-haul holidays Patagonia has become a
popular place for Welsh tourists. The Welsh descendants there
are only too happy to welcome them. In the villages are little
cottage tea rooms, where there is a continuous supply of Welsh
cakes. We were told they were much in demand for breakfast.
All very Welsh – but I was visibly shaken to see a signpost
directing motorists to Treorcki.

In 1991 the North Korean Communist Government were
anxious to take the opportunity to host the Inter-Parliamentary
Union Conference. Our first impression of Pyongyang was
one of spaciousness. It is a beautiful city set against a backdrop
of mountains. It is a city of trees, flowers, elegant fountains and
many winding waterways fringed with willows. It is also a city
of high-rise buildings but they are not oppressive as in Hong
Kong; the feeling of oppression comes from other sources.
Apart from public transport there was virtually no traffic, no
street furniture of any kind, no bicycles, prams or pushchairs,
no litter, no dogs or cats, no birds. There was no sign of life in
the flats; no washing was hung out to dry and no plants were
seen on the balconies. At main crossroads policemen stood
signalling to the scanty traffic and in the shops we were shown
around there were few consumer goods.

The whole city had a curiously blank air and after a time
each tree-lined street seemed much like any other – a case of
déjà vu. We were also puzzled by the absence of old people.
School children in attractive uniforms were frequently seen
marching in the streets singing purposefully. Sometimes voices
on loudspeakers were heard – music, too, varying from the
patriotic to the celestial. Wherever we went, there was an ever-
pervading presence of President Kim IL Sung whose pictures
dominated the city. He looked young and handsome, towering

above the smiling people. In fact he was in his early eighties at that time. He was small in stature, balding and frail. His name was invariably prefixed by 'our great leader' or 'our dear leader'.

The people were wonderfully well provided for. The showpiece of the city was a 600 room Grand People's Study House, built in traditional style with handsome curved grey-green roofs. It was in effect an enormous centre for adult education. We saw many people (some on day release) studying subjects of their choice in different rooms but there was an air of over-capacity.

Another day we were taken to a Schoolchildren's Palace, where, in the afternoons, children were able to pursue their special interests. These children were of the brightest and took delight in singing, dancing, music, painting, calligraphy, embroidery, boxing and the like. The instrumentalists in particular used identical gestures and facial expressions. Their professionalism went far beyond that which we would expect in a school open day in this country. It made one feel a little uneasy. A visit was arranged to a kindergarten where little ones were delighted for us to share their activities. It was explained to us that they were weekly boarders and returned home at the weekends. Their parents were said to be working and 'too busy' to look after them. Thinking I had misheard, I asked another interpreter. The reply – 'too busy' – was the same. Again, these appeared talented youngsters and they had been carefully coached for the visitors.

May Day dawned overcast and bitterly cold (as in Britain) but the people were determined not to allow the weather to mar their day's festivities. In a sedate pleasure park they feasted, danced and held competitions and games. Large groups spread out their picnics on the grass while cooking equipment was assembled to provide tasty fry-ups. Their kind hospitality was pressed on us, and we were able to join in their dancing.

The highlight of our visit was an entertainment in a vast stadium in which thousands of young people took part. But it was more than an entertainment – it was a spectacular affirmation of their way of life, a colourful feast of mass precision dancing, running, leaping. It was like a kaleidoscope changing design and colour every few minutes and all accompanied by loud patriotic music. At the back of the stadium, scenes of life in the city and beyond flashed before our eyes – these images were made up, mosaic-fashion, by people with 'books' of colours, which could be changed instantaneously to form moving pictures. There was an overwhelming exuberance to the spectacle and we watched – almost with disbelief – as the scenes unfolded. One slogan flashed before us. 'We are happy', the interpreter explained. Towards the end the arena was filled with young people forming a map of a united Korea and the audience rose to their feet. We could identify with their aspirations.

We were silent on leaving the stadium – the cultural shock was a bit much for us. By common agreement among the delegates, the conference was a great success. It is many years since our delegation to North Korea but even now I have a sense of privilege in having been able to visit this isolated and enigmatic country.

From 1991 to 1997, I served as the Welsh representative on the Council of Europe. The Leader of our delegation was Peter Hardy, MP Wentworth (now Lord Hardy of Wath). This body was established in 1949 and is quite distinct from the European Union. It has a permanent headquarters at the Palais de l'Europe in Strasbourg with a budget of approximately £152 million. When I stood down in 1997 it had forty-one European states as members, including fifteen countries from central and eastern Europe. Its aims can be summarised as follows:

to protect human rights and pluralist democracy

to promote awareness of a European cultural identity and
    encourage its development

to seek solutions to problems facing European society, e.g.
    environmental protection, AIDS, drugs and intolerance

to assist central and eastern European countries with their
    political, legislative and constitutional reforms

The Parliamentary Assembly met quarterly and I spoke occasionally in its debates. I also served on the Media Committee and sometimes we would take part in a foreign visit. One of these was to Vilnius, the capital of Lithuania, a most beautiful city but sadly neglected after so many years as part of the Soviet Union. Lithuania has a population of nearly four million, most of whom are Roman Catholics. Over many centuries (largely on account of its strategic position *vis-à-vis* East and West) it has accommodated people of many races and this is reflected in the large number of churches of different denominations. The cathedral is the focal point of the city and is very impressive. During the country's domination by the USSR, it was turned into an Art Gallery. Lithuania is a country that will prosper, given a peaceful and independent future.

A feature of the Council of Europe which I found interesting was that, in each weekly session of the Assembly, there is a VIP guest speaker. At the end of the speech there was always time for questions and I invariably participated. Once I crossed swords with Helmut Kohl, Chancellor of Germany, but he gave me a very reasonable reply and with a big smile on his face. Europeans take the Council of Europe very seriously but it is relatively unknown in Britain. This is regrettable because the Council is a very civilised body and, although largely a talking shop, it nevertheless does some useful work in bringing the people of Europe together.

CHAPTER 11

Westminster

ONE HEARS MUCH criticism of Government and of individual MPs but it has always surprised me how keen the general public are to visit Parliament. Over the years I have entertained many guests and parties from voluntary organisations, schools etc. A little ploy I developed was to keep my guests waiting for five or ten minutes in the Central Lobby. This is not out of any disrespect for my guests but what I have discovered is that, when I eventually meet up with them, I find they have been fascinated by the interesting people who have passed through the Lobby whilst they waited. There might have been well-known persons who are instantly recognisable, perhaps MPs from neighbouring constituencies and others whom they have seen on TV but cannot name. I have felt that this little interval helped to make their visit.

The tour of the Palace of Westminster begins in the Queen's Robing Room. It is here before opening Parliament that Her Majesty the Queen puts on the royal robes and the Imperial Crown. Legends of King Arthur adorn the walls. We then pass to the Royal Gallery where visiting statesmen may be invited to address both Houses of Parliament, as did President Reagan of the USA when Mrs Thatcher was Prime Minister. This visit, however, was not without controversy. At the time Michael Foot was Leader of the Labour Party and Mrs Thatcher was keen that the American President should speak in Westminster Hall which is the oldest and perhaps the most prestigious part of the Palace. The Labour Leader opposed this proposition, stating that President Reagan was not an important enough figure in history. In the event the President spoke in the Royal Gallery. The side walls there are adorned with two large pictures painted by Daniel Maclise. One shows the meeting of Wellington and Blucher after the Battle of Waterloo, and the other the death of Nelson at Trafalgar. The Prince's Chamber is said to be linked to the Black Prince, famous for his victory at the Battle of Crécy in 1346. This small ante-room is dominated by a giant marble statue of Queen Victoria. I usually point out that she reigned from 1837 to 1901, a total of sixty-four years and during such an important period in British history. Adorning the side wall is a portrait of Mary Queen of Scots and in the past I have tended to be rather coy about this famous lady because I knew so little about her. Recently, however, I have read Antonia Fraser's wonderful biography which gave me some new insights. What a tragic life she had after being, in early years, both Queen of Scotland and Queen of France (earlier marrying the Dauphin, who was someone equivalent to our Prince of Wales, i.e. heir to the throne).

In the House of Lords Chamber is enacted the most splendid of state occasions – the opening of Parliament, when the Sovereign reads to the assembled Lords and Commons the Speech from the Throne which sets out the Government's programme for the forthcoming session of Parliament. For me this ceremony tends to give rather a wrong impression of where power actually lies. The Prime Minister, who is responsible for the Gracious Speech, stands at the back of the Chamber like an innocent bystander, along with the Leader of the Opposition. Once I was standing with other MPs watching the ceremony and standing to the left of HM the Queen was Field Marshall Lord Montgomery, holding a sword aloft. As the proceedings got under way, I noticed the sword started to slip from the hands of the noble Lord and he passed out. He was about eighty at the time and the task proved to be too much even for a man of his steely determination.

Legislative sittings of the House of Lords are presided over by the Lord Chancellor who sits on the Woolsack with the mace behind him. He is rather an anomalous figure in the hierarchy of Government for, though he nominally presides over the Lords, it is essentially a self-regulating body. The Lord Chancellor is also head of the legal system and a member of the Cabinet. By contrast the Speaker of the House of Commons is divorced from Party politics and his or her sole task is to preside over the Lower Chamber of Parliament.

Some years ago there was a great crash during the deliberations of their Lordships. Almost without exception they dived under the benches, believing that a bomb had exploded. However, it turned out that one of the large chandeliers had crashed down from the ceiling, narrowly missing Lord Shinwell. Apparently the ceiling had begun to suffer from dry rot on account of the central heating. Lord Shinwell was unharmed and I should point out that he went on to live until he was over a hundred.

In the Central Lobby, where visitors and constituents wait for Members of Parliament, can be seen the mosaics representing St George, St Andrew, St Patrick and, as I put it, our own St David. The visitor then passes along the corridor to the Members' Lobby, taking the same route as Black Rod takes when summoning the Commons to the Lords at the opening of Parliament. At the entrance of the House of Commons chamber are two famous statues, one of Sir Winston Churchill, Prime Minister during the Second World War, and the other of David Lloyd George (subsequently Earl Lloyd George of Dwyfor), who presided over the nation's destiny at the time of the First World War. Visitors over the years have rubbed Churchill's shoe so that the black outer colour has been replaced by a shiny brassy effect.

For people visiting from the provinces, a day out in London can be a very tiring business. Children in particular often sit

down in the Chamber, whereupon a burly policeman will
shout, 'Stand up'. I tell the kids that once when Ted Heath was
Prime Minister, following a visit of a party of school children a
pool of water was discovered under his seat. Since then I point
out no visitor has been allowed to sit in the Chamber. One of
the traditions kept up is the red lines separating Members on
the front bench below the gangway. They are a sword-length
apart, a legacy, I suppose, of when the wearing of swords was
commonplace.

A feature of the Parliamentary week is Prime Minister's
Questions and gallery tickets are very difficult to obtain. Until
1997 these sessions were held from 3.15 p.m. to 3.30 p.m. each
Tuesday and Thursday but when Tony Blair became Prime
Minister the arrangement was changed and now they are held
for half an hour each Wednesday from 12.00 p.m. to 12.30 p.m.

I think visitors to the Chamber come away with two
overwhelming impressions, firstly the extreme austerity of the
place and secondly its smallness. Indeed there is not enough
room to accommodate all MPs at the same time. A tour of the
Palace of Westminster would usually conclude with a visit to
Westminster Hall which is steeped in history. It is the only
major part of the ancient Palace which survives in its original
form. The stark stone floor, together with the hammer-beam
roof, leaves a lasting impression even on a casual visitor. Tablets
on the floor of the Hall commemorate the lying-in-state of Mr
Gladstone in 1898, of King Edward VII in 1910, of George V in
1936, of King George VI in 1952, of Queen Mary in 1953 and
of Sir Winston Churchill in 1965. It was the venue for the
Royal Courts of Justice until 1882 and it was here that the trials
took place of many notabilities including Charles I, Sir
Thomas More and the infamous Guy Fawkes.

One of the highlights while visiting Westminster Hall is to
take a quick look into the Crypt Chapel, properly known as the
Chapel of St Mary Undercroft. It is approached by some steps

in the corner of the Hall. It has an ornate eye-catching appearance with a slightly foreign look. Allegedly, at one stage of our history with fierce religious differences, it was turned into a stable and its walls whitewashed. Nowadays it can be used by Parliamentarians and their families for baptisms, marriages and memorial services and is a regular place of worship for all those whose lives revolve round the Palace of Westminster.

I am reminded of an English colleague who once told me about two ladies who had come to London for a day out. After completing their tour of the Palace of Westminster, one said to the other, 'What shall we do now, May?'

The reply was 'Let's go to the cinema.'

'What's on?'

'Moby Dick.'

'I don't like those ol' sex films.'

'No, it's not about sex. It's about whales.'

'Oh, I don't like those Welsh buggers either.'

As a member of a minority race in the UK, I suppose I have to take these little jokes in my stride.

Another feature of a visit to Parliament is the Speaker's procession which takes place immediately before the House of Commons commences at 2.30 p.m. When George Thomas (Viscount Tonypandy) was Speaker he would sometimes give a wink as he passed through the assembled crowd in the Central Lobby. It is rather impressive to see the Speaker in his full regalia with the Sergeant-at-Arms bearing the mace and the train-bearers following behind. The House of Commons, of course, cannot transact any business until the mace is in place. There have been one or two incidents over the years when an irate Member has picked up the mace and the House is automatically dissolved. Immediately before Questions begin there are prayers for approximately five minutes, led by the Speaker's Chaplain. In the House of Lords twenty-six Church of England Bishops sit, including the Archbishop of Canterbury, and they seem to take it in turn to say prayers.

At certain times a Division is called and then the bells ring. They wake the dead, as I sometimes say. Two ladies were once present in the Central Lobby when the ringing began. They were quite alarmed and one said to the other, 'What's happened?' The reply was 'I think one of them must have escaped!'

When I had a school party in the Commons Chamber I would ask the question 'How old do you think this Chamber is?' Invariably the reply would come forth – perhaps three, four or five hundred years. I would proceed to point out that the Chamber was destroyed by enemy bombing during the Second World War. MPs then sat in the House of Lords Chamber and their Lordships were consigned to a committee room. When it was rebuilt after the war Churchill was instrumental in ensuring that the new Chamber still had the cross-party design, whereas legislative chambers on the continent tend to be circular in shape. He believed that when a Member changed Party he should cross the floor and not just slide around as would happen in a circular Chamber. I should point out that Churchill was quite an authority on these matters, having changed Party three or four times!

In 1974 the northern end of Westminster Hall was severely damaged by fire following a terrorist bomb attack. At the time in this area I shared an office with Professor John Mackintosh[*] but fortunately I was away when the explosion occurred. Just outside is the underground car park provided for Members and it was here that Airey Neave lost his life while driving his car down to the park.

It has been customary over many years in the House of Commons to have a Welsh Day debate some time near St

---

[*]Late MP East Lothian.

David's Day. The debate invariably ranges far and wide, for it provides an opportunity for individual Welsh MPs to air their particular grievances at the time. During the thirty-one years I spent in the Commons I regularly took part in this debate. One that particularly stands out in my memory was the debate held on 10 February 1983. The economy was in deep depression and in usually prosperous Newport male unemployment stood at 18.8 per cent. I made a particularly rumbustious contribution and in the Hansard official report (Col.1218) my opening remarks are quoted as follows:

> Mr Roy Hughes (Newport): Even longer than ten years ago, but more particularly in the 1975 Common Market referendum campaign, the hon. Member for Flint West (Sir A. Meyer) and others were painting a vision of the Common Market in which hundreds of thousands of new jobs would be created – a bonanza in which Wales would be joining. Instead, we have suffered an avalanche of manufactured imported goods. The floodgates have been opened. We are paying for many of those goods with North Sea revenues. In the process, our own people are being put on the dole. The Common Market itself, as a trading entity, now has an unemployment level of twelve million.
>
> All that the House heard today from the hon. Member for Flint West was gloom and doom. His remarks show how the hon. Gentleman and many of his colleagues misled the British people. Wales is suffering from unemployment worse than that of the 1930s. At that time its people could move to places like Birmingham. To paraphrase the Secretary of State for Employment who is well known for his literacy, people could get on their bikes. Now, however, the Midlands is becoming an industrial wasteland. Unemployment is engulfing most of the country. Even the southeast of England has an unemployment level of about ten per cent.

Later on I called for the revival of the idea of an iron ore terminal for Llanwern. The lack of such a facility has been the essential difference between the Margam works at Port Talbot and Llanwern. If Ministers and steel chiefs had had the vision to see this, then I have little doubt that Llanwern would still be making steel well into the twenty-first century. Llanwern already had the advantage of being better placed on the eastern seaboard and therefore more accessible to markets.

At 9.41 p.m. the Under-Secretary of State for Wales (Mr Michael Roberts) rose to reply to the debate (Hansard col. 1230-1). Three minutes later he passed the question to me. 'I wonder whether the hon. Member for Newport Mr Hughes, will explain how much of that (Japanese) industry he expects to see coming into Wales with all the inducements that he and some of his hon. Friends might offer if Britain, including Wales, is outside the Common Market. If he does not wish to give that explanation perhaps the hon. Gentleman . . .'

At that moment he dramatically collapsed at the despatch box. The Deputy Speaker Mr Ernest Armstrong was in the chair and he suspended the sitting immediately. Dr Roger Thomas (Carmarthen) attended poor Michael on the floor of the Chamber but alas his efforts were of no avail.

Michael Roberts came from a distinguished Welsh family. He was a devout Tory; very sociable, particularly at the bar. His death raised the question of the widely held belief that people are 'not allowed' to die in the Palace of Westminster. The Library of the House of Lords supplied me with the following explanation:

'It is generally the practice to assume, in the case of a person who is suddenly taken ill in the Palace of Westminster and subsequently dies, that the actual point of death occurs outside the Precincts of the Palace of Westminster.'

I suspect this is probably because there is some doubt as to how any Inquest might take place on a death in the Palace. Under the Coroners Act of 1887 there is some question as to whether the district coroner for Westminster would have jurisdiction over a death occurring in the Palace, since deaths in Royal Palaces are reserved for the jurisdiction of the Coroner of the Queen's Household. The likelihood would be that a long and cumbersome legal procedure would ensue. It is therefore thought simpler to assume the death took place outside the Palace, such that any inquest or investigation might be carried out in the normal way and unnecessary aggravation of distress of the relatives etc. be avoided.

Each Friday morning when Parliament is in session every member of the Commons and the Lords receives 'The Whip'. This document sets out the business for the following week. The importance of the issues to be debated is indicated by lines under each item e.g. 'One Line' means it is very unlikely there will be a vote. 'Two Lines' means there might be one and 'Three Lines' means a real Party controversial issue and attendance is mandatory. Also on the Whip are details of the various meetings that will be held the following week and they range far and wide.

During my time in the Commons 'Pairing' was very much the vogue. From 1982 to 1997 my 'Pair' was Sir Peter Fry, the Conservative Member for Wellingborough in Northampton-shire. Peter became a good friend. We had a mutual love of rugby and formed in Parliament 'The All Party Rugby Union Group' and this was helpful because an All Party Rugby League Group was already in existence and quite active.

Our main linkage, though, was through Road Transport because from 1982 to 1997 we were Joint Chairmen of the All Party Roads Study Group. For the same period I also served on the Public Policy Committee of the Royal Automobile Club (RAC). This was quite a prestigious body and serving on it were retired former Permanent Secretaries, some leading figures from industry and the immediately retired Head of the Metropolitan Police. Earlier I had been Parliamentary Private Secretary to Mr Fred Mulley MP, when he was Minister for Transport.

With the Lord Mayor of Coventry, Councillor Geoff White, and the Lady Mayoress, together with my 'pair' in the Commons, Sir Peter Fry MP.

The 'Roads Group' was one of the oldest of its kind in Parliament. It was founded in 1956 and over the years it met regularly and at these meetings presentations were made to MPs and Peers. Funding came from bodies linked to the motor industry such as the British Road Federation, the AA, RAC, Society of Motor Manufacturers and Traders (SMMT), the Road Haulage Association and others. They came together in a body known as the Roads Campaign Council which was chaired by the redoubtable Jack Williams, who was popular with both Labour and Conservative Members. Earlier I had also joined the All Party Motor Industry Group and for ten years I was joint Chairman of that body, besides serving beforehand as Vice-chairman, when my good colleague, George Park (Coventry East), was Chairman.

The gatherings organised by the Roads and Motors Groups were pleasant occasions and quite a camaraderie was built up.

For some years Arthur Butler and Frank Richardson acted as the secretariat for the Roads Group and they did a first class job. We had an annual overseas trip to see various road network schemes in different parts of the world. In my capacity as Joint Chairman of the Motor Industry Group, I found that numerous international companies were keen to receive delegations. Thus we went to Detroit to see the General Motors operation and to the Soviet Union to see Lada. Saab invited us to their plants in both Sweden and Finland while Volkswagen received us in Wolfberg and Fiat in Italy. My friends, Bernard Conlan (Gateshead) and David Marshall (Glasgow Shettleston), regularly took part in these visits. In both Groups I largely had responsibility for selecting the Labour delegates.

Paul Murphy (Torfaen), after he entered the House in 1987, became active in both Groups and this was understandable because motor component companies were the major employer of labour in his constituency. He joined us on several overseas delegations. He is the present Secretary of State for Northern Ireland.

My experience as Joint Chairman of both the Roads Group and the Motor Industry Group gave me a most valuable insight into the nation's transport system. What has amazed me over the years is how ill-informed so many people are about transport matters. There is an insufficient realisation of the fact that over ninety per cent of passenger and freight transport is by road, which makes Britain very much a road-based economy. There has been a naive belief that we should not build any more roads or even properly maintain our existing network but instead people and freight should go by rail. Now rail is a wonderful form of travel, normally safe and environmentally friendly. What is not fully appreciated is that Beeching decimated our rail network forty years ago and what is left of it has been starved of investment, particularly during the Thatcher era. The Labour Government from 1997 to 2001 made a serious attempt to put more passengers and freight back on rail. Despite new investment, the attempt has put extra pressure on rail, leading to a number of disasters and relative chaos regarding timetables.

Ordinary people tend to love their motor cars which have become vital for travelling to and from work, while for drivers going to out-of-town supermarkets, a car is invaluable. So much of the countryside and various beauty spots are opened to the general public because of new roads. Private transport was once the prerogative of the rich but with the car this provision has been widely extended.

It is simple common sense, however, that we cannot indefinitely put more cars on the road, for eventually we would become gridlocked. People must be persuaded to use their cars less and rely more on public transport. What point is there, though, when in some areas, particularly in the countryside, public transport is virtually non-existent. Governments, then, have to invest heavily in providing efficient public transport in order to get a response to their call to leave the car at home.

In each session of Parliament Members have the opportunity to introduce Private Members' Bills. As only six such Bills have a chance of becoming law in view of time restrictions, I was fortunate to get a high place in the lottery. In 1991 I was chosen and I received a number of letters from various organisations requesting me to put forward a Bill to further their cause. I finally decided that my Bill should be for the protection of badgers. This was an issue of particular concern to residents in South East Wales where we lived, as the thick woodlands made ideal homes for badgers. The object of the Bill was to block loopholes in the present legislation. Badgers had been protected for more than twenty years but not their homes. Prosecutions against baiters had failed as they could plead that their dogs were ferreting out foxes in 'disused' setts.

In the *South Wales Argus* (7 February 1991) the editorial reported 'It is hard for us to imagine that any MP will want to oppose this sensible extension of the law which will give further protection to one of nature's most shy, yet most beautiful creatures'. Throughout my campaign I was indebted to the League Against Cruel Sports for advising me through the intricacies of the Bill (not as straightforward as might be imagined). I also received much support from badger groups throughout the country and other societies promoting animal welfare. I have, too, a letter from Ted Heath supporting the Bill, and also one from Winston Churchill. Phil Drabble, the well-known BBC reporter on sheepdog trials, also wrote to me.

The First Reading of the Bill is a formality, the real test coming in the Second Reading debate. This takes place on a Friday when MPs are anxious to leave Westminster and return to their constituencies. It is necessary for one hundred Members to vote for the Bill before it can proceed. In this I was fortunate as exactly one hundred Members voted for it, with nineteen against. One fewer vote for the Bill would have seen its collapse.

The Bill then proceeded to the House of Lords where, in the capable hands of the late Lord Houghton, a long-time fighter for animal welfare, it passed its necessary stages and came back to the Commons for final approval.

I was particularly pleased to see in Hansard (10 May 1991) a contribution by Sir Alan Glyn (Conservative, Windsor and Maidenhead) – 'Many of my constituents love badgers. Tonight, I shall be joining the badgers at the bottom of my garden, in celebrating the passage of the Bill. The toast will be "The hon. Member for Newport East".'

CHAPTER 12

Electioneering

MANY YEARS AGO when I was Secretary of Pontllanfraith Labour Party, the Treasurer was a man called Bert Brown. He worked as a representative of the Pearl Insurance Company but he was not the type we have today who pick up substantial endowment payments on a quarterly or annual basis. Bert Brown went around the doors collecting very small amounts which were invariably earmarked for providing a respectable burial at some future date. One thing he taught me was 'In an election, hold a candle to the devil'. I took this to heart and it served me well in Newport, as my election results indicate. When I canvassed, however unrealistic the views of some people might be, I always argued that it was all the more reason why they should vote Labour. Once Lady Soskice, the wife of my predecessor, was canvassing down in Pill, the dock area of Newport. She knocked on a door and a big burly man answered. 'I am canvassing for Sir Frank Soskice,' she said. 'Could I count on your vote?'

'I don't care who you are,' the man replied, 'I'm voting Labour.'

Electioneering for me was a family business and spent on the streets, knocking on doors. It was a real presence – better than all your telephone canvassing. Marion was always there, together with our three girls, who were all decked out in red outfits, as they wore when supporting Wales at Cardiff Arms Park. Meriel, the youngest, began canvassing at a very tender age. One day she knocked on a door in the Malpas area of Newport and said, 'I am canvassing for Mr Roy Hughes, the

Labour candidate. Can we count on your support?' The man answered rather aggressively 'Oh, I don't know what I am doing and anyway who are you?'

Meriel replied, 'I am Roy Hughes' daughter'. The man changed his tune instantly and said, 'I always vote Labour and here's 10p for you.'

There was a man in Blaen-y-Pant Avenue who was persistently writing letters to the *South Wales Argus* attacking me for the stand I had taken on various policy issues. Rosemary, my eldest daughter, inadvertently knocked on his door and politely asked if he would be supporting Mr Roy Hughes this time. 'Do you think I am mad?' he fumed, frightening the poor girl out of her wits. Pamela and Meriel once got entangled with Gerald Davies, a Conservative candidate in the 1979 General Election. He threatened to report them for harassment to Roy Hughes' agent.

My brother Granville is a sort of armchair Scargillite but in one General Election I persuaded him and his brother-in-law, Ifor Gravenor, to come down to Newport to help on election night. I left them in St Julians Ward and in the capable hands of Mrs Marjorie Scott JP, one of the great loyalists of Newport Labour Party. It was a wet day and they picked up a rather elderly lady to take her to the polling station. She got in the car and my brother Granville slammed the door, breaking her umbrella in half. I have often wondered if that lady voted Labour. One advantage of Granville's assistance in this way was that we are rather alike in appearance and, if voters thought Granville was me, he did not disabuse them.

In elections to canvass and distribute literature a good deal of voluntary help is needed. In the Newport constituency and later Newport East, the Constituency Secretary, Councillor Ken Powell, always worked very hard. My agent in several elections was County Councillor Dick Murray, a great character. He brought all the wit and charm of his native

Dublin to the scene and it was a pleasure to be in his company. A devout Catholic, tragically Dick died very suddenly of a heart attack. This was at a time when he was about to be made a Knight of the Church and Vice-Chairman of Gwent County Council, whereupon he would have become Chairman the following year. We had planned to visit Ireland when he took up office because he was well acquainted with the political scene and knew most of the leading figures. Alas . . .

After a gruelling election campaign over a period of some four weeks, the atmosphere at the count was always friendly and tranquil. There was, however, an exception in 1979 for we had a National Front candidate in Newport. At the count they had a small group of bully boys who were allowed to attend as tellers, and they were intent on disrupting the proceedings. One kept on treading on my foot and I was rather embarrassed, for I did not know how best to react to such provocation. Eventually I approached the Police Officer who was present to ensure that the proceedings were conducted in an orderly manner. He said, 'Mr Hughes, I can get them evicted but there will be quite a disruption, which is just what they want in order to get publicity.' I agreed with him, so I kept out of the way as far as I could and the count proceeded, at least without any major disorder.

In speaking of Fascists I recall an incident in Blackpool, at the 1965 Labour Party Conference. Ray Gunter, originally from Abertillery, was in the Chair and an education debate was in progress. I was anxious to speak in this debate and I stood up holding my conference agenda in the air when Ray Gunter put out his arm and said, 'Sit down, boy'. At that very instant Colin Jordan, Leader of the National Front, jumped on to the rostrum giving the Nazi salute. He had somehow managed to inveigle his way into Conference but he was quickly ousted by the stewards. The appearance of a National Front candidate in Newport was directly related to the fact that we had an immigrant community, largely from Pakistan. During the election campaign I would visit a mosque, take off my shoes and proceed to give the assembled gathering a little talk on what the Labour Party stood for. I was always received in a very friendly fashion. From time to time members of the Pakistani community came to my constituency surgery and I helped them whenever I could. Throughout my thirty-one years representing Newport I can never recall raising the issue of race on the floor of the House of Commons, for I felt this would have been counterproductive. I am glad to say that over the years there has been little racial tension in the town.

Normally during a General Election campaign we held an Eve of the Poll rally at Transport House on the Cardiff Road. I would speak last to try and rally the faithful, emphasising the rightness of our cause and urging them to get out and vote the following day. On one occasion I returned to the meeting hall to find people standing outside. I could not make this out and thought that possibly the meeting had finished early. In the event it was a bomb scare that had emptied the hall. Some of us retired to the Irish Club just around the corner, where we had a splendid welcome and all said they intended to vote Labour.

Every ten to fifteen years the Boundary Commissioners come into action to make any adjustments to constituency boundaries which may be necessary, bearing in mind movement in population and other anomalies. In Wales the average constituency numbers about 57,000 voters. Here we have a separate commission and not long before the 1983 General Election it put forward its final recommendations.

The Abertillery constituency as such was abolished, while Newport was to be enlarged and then divided into two seats, East and West. Over the years with pit closures and the ending of steel-making at Ebbw Vale, people tended to drift down the valley to the coastal strip to find new employment. There was much opposition to these proposals and I seem to recall that, when Margaret Thatcher called the General Election, Newport Labour Party had not formally accepted the new boundaries. I opted for Newport East although there was little difference between the two seats from a political standpoint. Monmouth constituency, which was Tory held, had already chosen a candidate when the boundary changes were announced, but as some of the area making up the new Newport East constituency embraced part of what had previously been Monmouth constituency, the candidate there exercised his right to be nominated for Newport East. In the event at a selection conference I won easily by eighty votes to seven.

The dissolution of the old Newport Labour Party was a sad and nostalgic evening for us all. Memories crowded in on us as we recalled the electoral battles fought and won over the years and the comradeship generated and sustained throughout that time. In the change around I lost some wonderful workers e.g. Councillor Mrs Bosley and Councillor Mrs Kehmstedt, both subsequently Mayors of Newport. There was Mrs Mogford Jones, Treasurer of the Party and a real skinflint one at that. Then there was my good friend Councillor Stewart Watson, Leader of the Council and a most loyal character. Locally I recall the valuable assistance given by the local Councillors who knew their wards intimately.

The new Newport East constituency took in Caldicot, a small town which flourished first by its proximity to the Llanwern steelworks and later with the Second Severn Crossing. In Caldicot was the solid presence of Councillor Graham Powell with all his vast experience. The local Councillors engaged in a good deal of repartee with the people they represented. Children clustered around when they knew we had stickers to give out and posters to distribute. Sometimes we were joined by helpers who could only stay a short time but whose help was nevertheless much valued.

'Sorry I must go now and get the children their dinner' or 'I must go now. I'm on afternoons this week.'

An area new to us was Llanmartin, a quiet backwater a few miles from Newport. The local community councillors, led by the redoubtable John Murphy, met us and took us around the district several times. A community spirit had been fostered there which matched that of the valleys. Llanmartin had been built to house an influx of workers at the nearby Llanwern steelworks. The social mix was interesting. The Ward Councillor, Garfield Mathias, came from the Rhondda, John Murphy, the Ward Secretary, had come down from Scotland and Mrs Howells, a Community Councillor who cared for the elderly, was from Llanelli. During the campaign we talked to many old people who were anxious to have a chat with us. We visited several complexes for pensioners and the residents were proud to show us their palaces with their china cabinets and family photographs.

Our daughters also assisted us. Meriel, the youngest, who was at that time 'festering', as it is called, in the Lower Sixth, joined us in Newport when possible, while Pamela two years older, a student in London, appeared late one night unannounced and stayed a few days to help, while our eldest daughter, Rosemary, a teacher in Inner London, spent her half term holiday with us. She threw her energies into the campaign and her flair for publicity was invaluable.

Then came the count. We had been watching the results* as they came out on the TV and soon realised the worst was happening. Throughout the country the opposition vote was divided, giving the Conservatives a runaway victory. Newport West fell to the Conservatives. There was much tension in the Ringland Leisure Centre as the votes were counted. At last the result came and the figures were as follows:

---

*The 1983 General Election.

Hughes R.J. (Lab)	15,931
Thomason R. (Cons)	13,301
David Ms F. (SDP/All)	10,293
Thomas D. (Plaid)	697
Labour majority	2,630

The 1983 General election in my new constituency of Newport East proved to be the most difficult of the eight Parliamentary contests I took part in. However, one of my favourite sayings is 'Survival is the name of the game.'

CHAPTER 13

The Second Severn Crossing

WITH A BACKGROUND in transport and living in Chepstow, it was understandable, I suppose, that I became interested in the Severn Crossing. From earliest times efforts have been made to provide an easy link between one side of the Severn and the other. The Severn Tunnel was completed in 1884 after many setbacks and as a result the river was without a ferry service for forty years with the exception of a few small boats. A service started up again in 1926-27 at the time of the General Strike when food was ferried across for striking miners. Later, during the great depression, interest waned in the ferry and it had to close for twelve to eighteen months. In August 1931 Mr Enoch Williams inaugurated a new service and it seems to have been well patronised until the time when the first Severn Bridge was opened in September 1966. This was six months after I was first elected to Parliament.

This bridge is really part of the London-South Wales Motorway (M4). It crosses the River Severn between Aust on the English side and Beachley on the Welsh side. It was built for the Ministry of Transport and the Joint Consulting Engineers were Mott, Hay and Anderson, and Freeman, Fox and Partners. The substructure was built by John Howard & Co Ltd and the superstructure by Associated Bridge Builders, a combine of three companies, Sir William Arrol and Co Ltd, Cleveland Bridge and Engineering Co Ltd and Dorman Long (Bridge & Engineering Ltd). The bridge is a suspension one and the latest techniques in design and construction were employed. It was the second largest bridge in Europe, ranking after the Forth Road Bridge, which was also built by Associated Bridge Builders. The first part of the construction programme began in 1961 and five years later it was opened. It was much admired at the time. People were proud of it and felt it was a fine example of British engineering and construction. It was both handsome and elegant but was nevertheless plagued by rust and ricketiness almost as soon as it was opened. Lane closures soon became a feature, for its economic success overloaded it with traffic at peak times. These difficulties were evident, despite the immediate benefits brought to both sides of the Severn. South Wales manufacturers could transport their goods to England much more cheaply and companies in the Midlands and Southern England found similar benefits.

Cultural and social ties were enhanced. People could travel from South Wales to Bristol to go to the theatre without a fifty mile detour via Gloucester. Tourism benefited and day trips to Wales became a regular feature for English families. The plain fact, too, was that without the bridge and the motorway it carried, many industries just would not have come to Wales. For myself, brought up in the South Wales mining valleys with distant memories of economic depression, it was this fact that made the bridge so important. My political philosophy could be summed up very simply, inasmuch as people need a decent job to give them pride and dignity which could lead to happiness and prosperity. People out of work soon become depressed and demoralised. In economic terms unemployment is sheer waste, like a tap left running. It was with these thoughts in mind that I latched on to the issue of the Severn Crossing and I pursued it week in, week out, year in, year out.

From the start the bridge bore a toll charge but there had, I understand, been some objection to this imposition. Mr Ness Edwards (MP Caerphilly) was, I believe, an influential voice in opposition to the whole principle of tolls. The charge was introduced, however, at half a crown (twelve and a half pence) and such was the elation at the benefits accruing that this charge passed without too much controversy. There was a feeling that at last the whole problem of crossing the Severn had been conquered.

In 1979, however, the charge was raised to twenty pence for cars and forty pence for lorries. From then on the whole situation was exacerbated because for the next four years there were perpetual restrictions on traffic on the bridge. On 5 November 1983 *The Times* listed the troubles:

October 1979: Lane closures and a thirty mile per hour limit for three weeks for resurfacing.

November 1979: Brief lane closures to allow replacement of hangers joining the deck to the main suspension cables.

April 1980: Further surface patching for two weeks. Lane closures and a thirty m.p.h. limit.

October 1980: A three month project to replace more hangers. Lane closures in daylight initially, followed by overnight lane closures.

June 1981: Daytime lane closures until mid-July for hanger replacements.

October 1981: Phase two of the same operation.

February 1982: Early morning lane closures after tests indicated that the strength of some hangers might not give an acceptable margin of safety under extreme traffic conditions.

October 1982: Lane closures and a thirty m.p.h. limit during three weeks of patching the road surface.

October 10 1983: More road surface patching and the start of hanger replacements. Lane closures and a thirty mph limit.

October: Mrs Lynda Chalker, Minister of State for Transport, announces an extension of the early morning restrictions imposed in February 1982.

In 1983 the Department of Transport brought forward a

proposal to increase tolls for cars to fifty pence and for lorries to be charged one pound. This meant an increase of 150 per cent which was not very acceptable to ordinary motorists or road haulage interests. The simple economic principle that I have adhered to is that when you increase the cost of transport you increase the cost of just about everything. The proposals before implementation could be challenged at a public hearing. For my part I took the opportunity to seek an Adjournment debate in the House of Commons, with the object of making my opposition crystal clear. It was at this time that manna came down from heaven, for I got my hands on a hitherto secret report which clearly indicated that the bridge was in bad shape.

I secured an Adjournment debate on Friday 28 October 1983 and such a debate takes place after all other business has been concluded. It was a wet Friday afternoon and there were only three people in the Chamber – Mr Ernest Armstrong, Deputy Speaker, Mrs Lynda Chalker, Minister of State, Department of Transport, and myself. I rose to speak at 2.04 p.m. (Hansard col. 593):

> I am glad to have this opportunity to raise the proposal to increase tolls on the Severn Bridge by 150 per cent. Needless to say, there has been a storm of protest throughout South Wales about it. Gwent County Council, Newport Borough Council, the Newport and Gwent Chamber of Commerce, the AA and the RAC have all protested. Those protests are understandable because the motoring public are already being soaked by reason of the extortionist attitude of the Government. On the one hand, the amount collected from tolls is a mere pittance; on the other hand the collection causes delay and disrupts the traffic.
>
> It makes no sense to pay a toll for a short stretch of motorway, even if it happens to be across an estuary, for the rest of the motoring network is funded out of the public purse. Moreover, the Severn Bridge tolls are an inhibiting factor to the development of the Welsh economy, and new enterprises think twice before going to Wales.

In normal circumstances there is no logical justification for tolls. However, the circumstances of this bridge are not normal. Indeed, the state of the bridge is the main argument that I wish to put forward against the proposal to increase tolls, and certainly the state of the bridge is giving cause for anxiety.

I have repeatedly stressed in the House, in speeches and parliamentary questions and in letters to Ministers, the importance of this bridge to the Welsh economy. In some quarters doubts have been expressed about its safety. Some of us have been reluctant to enlarge on that aspect for fear of damaging business prospects.

I then went on to read out large sections of the report by the eminent firm of Consulting Engineers Mott, Hay and Anderson. The report was submitted to the Flint and Neill Partnership who in turn were acting on behalf of the Department of Transport.

Of course, the report went into great detail. The overall picture it presented was one of alarm. Basically, on present day loading, it was found that the vital components such as the towers, saddles and hangers were seriously overstressed. The hangers in particular caused concern, as they were vulnerable to progressive failure under relatively short traffic jams, if the weight of traffic exceeded about 700 tonnes over a stretch of about 200 metres of the bridge. The towers, too, were found to be vulnerable to extreme wind conditions. There might be warning of impending failure of the hanger system and other parts at risk, but not of the towers. All the stresses caused by overloading were, of course, exacerbated (particularly on the towers) by winds and it was recommended that the bridge should be closed to all traffic whenever winds of seventy m.p.h. or more were forecast, and that the bridge should be closed to all traffic immediately if a traffic jam should develop in storm conditions.

The Minister in her reply dealt with the issue of the

proposed toll increase, saying that the Government's policy was 'well known, if not widely understood. It was that expensive estuarial crossings should be paid for by those who used it rather than by taxpayers or ratepayers . . . No one can argue that the users of estuarial crossings do not benefit in time and in money from the shorter routes provided. It is these benefits which drivers pay towards when they choose to travel on the tolled crossings instead of going by the shortest alternative routes.'

The Minister then went on to say:

> There is no danger of the bridge being overloaded by traffic in normal free-flow conditions, but such overloading could occur if there were a build-up of closely spaced heavy lorries following, for example, a breakdown or accident on the bridge. The appraisal revealed also that certain components of the bridge had reduced margins of safety in respect of other load effects, notably wind. In addition, there has been an increased incidence of fatigue and/or corrosion in certain components, such as the hangers and deck plates . . . The large increase in the volume of very heavy lorries which was not foreseen when the crossing was designed in the 1950s is one of the main factors to consider. For avoidance of doubt, I point out that what is at issue is not the weight of individual lorries but the total weight of traffic on a particular length. The crossing was designed to the then British Standard 153 which was first issued in 1954. That standard has been superseded by British standard 5400. However, recent extensive statistical studies have shown that even British standard 5400 considerably underestimates the extreme loadings which can occur if traffic, including a high proportion of heavy goods vehicles, builds up and comes to a standstill. In our view, it is correct to guard against these extreme but possible conditions. The increase in the total weight of traffic using the crossing has been a contributory factor in the increased incidence of fatigue in certain components . . . The Flint and Neill report, published in May 1983 which referred to the feasibility study, concluded that it

was technically feasible to strengthen the crossing so that it could carry, without restriction, the flow of traffic and considerably heavier loads than at present. The total cost at current prices was estimated to be £33 million, of which £5 million would be for major maintenance work.

Here I should point out that, in the event, approximately eighty million pounds was spent on this work to strengthen the crossing. Mrs Chalker conceded, too, that she was not saying that the concern which had been stirred by the debate was unfounded 'because we are all concerned about the bridge but people should not fear using it.'

Nevertheless, two days later (30 October) Mrs Chalker ordered immediate restrictions – one lane only in each direction, twenty-four hours a day, five days a week. (There are not so many heavy lorries on the bridge at weekends).

I have always been an admirer of Lynda Chalker and felt she should have been made Minister of Transport. Apparently, however, with Mrs Thatcher as Prime Minister, there could only be one Queen Bee.

In my Adjournment debate the Minister was undoubtedly at a disadvantage without knowing that I was going to make such extensive use of a hitherto secret report. In the back of my mind I was motivated by several factors. Firstly, there was the tragedy of Aberfan which occurred because the authorities were not pressed hard enough to take remedial action early on. Such action could have prevented a terrible loss of life. Secondly, efficient transport links to London and the South East of England are absolutely vital to the economy of South Wales. The parlous state of the Severn Bridge caused much difficulty. Thirdly, it was a means of expediting a Government decision on a Second Crossing. There were, however, several years of campaigning ahead, which to some extent I enjoyed because I realised the importance of the cause. I knew that public opinion was on our side. It was this Adjournment debate and the report which was unveiled that gave the impetus to the campaign for a Second Crossing.

The Welsh media gave excellent support. The *South Wales Argus, Western Mail, Echo* and the weekly newspapers all played their part, as did the BBC and HTV. There was considerable interest, too, in the national press. *The Times* devoted many column inches to the issue and it was also well reported in the *Financial Times* and *The Economist. The Guardian* newspaper on 29 October printed an article headed '"Severn Bridge could collapse in strong wind", say engineers.'

On the following Monday, John Prescott MP, who was then Shadow Minister of Transport, put in a Standing Order 9 request in the Commons to obtain an emergency statement from the Minister. Nicholas Ridley MP, the Secretary of State for Transport in his reply accused me of being 'alarmist', yet immediately after my Adjournment debate restrictions were increased from that evening to twenty-four hours a day. (Hansard col. 747). Mr James Callaghan MP, the former Prime Minister, said, 'I do not think that the public will be totally reassured by the Minister's statement.' He went on to say that it was time to begin the preparations for a second bridge. (Col.748). My colleague, Barry Jones MP, (Alyn & Deeside) the Shadow Secretary of State for Wales said, 'If the Minister had been as conscientious in this as my hon. Friend the Member for Newport East (Mr Hughes), this mess would not have arisen. The Minister's remarks about my hon. Friend were disgraceful and they will not be well received in Wales.'

There was considerable interest at the Welsh Labour Group meeting held on 1 November and a decision was taken to seek an early meeting with the Secretary of State for Transport, Mr Nicholas Ridley. Mr Brynmor John MP (Pontypridd) was Chairman of our group at the time and on 10 November he led the delegation to the Department of Transport. We called for the speeding up of the repair and strengthening work on the bridge, and an early decision about the construction of a second crossing. The Minister largely rebuffed our call for a new bridge and said he was just not going 'to dig another hole in the ground'. Earlier the Government's attitude had been made clear by his predecessor, Mr Tom King MP, who indicated that there was not going to be any new construction at least until the early years of the next century and only then if it was found to be necessary.

Soon a campaign began which united all sections of public opinion throughout Wales. People had come to realise the importance of the Severn Estuary link-up and the unreliability of the existing bridge. On Monday 28 November, the CBI called a major conference in Cardiff. Private and public sections of industry were represented, together with Local Government, the Trade Unions, MPs and other interested parties. A further large conference was organised by Gwent County Council on January 1984. I spoke at both meetings. Decisions were taken, calling on the Government to speed up the strengthening and maintenance work, in addition to an early feasibility study for a second crossing. I continued to campaign in Parliamentary Questions, speeches, letters and articles in the press, and through television and radio interviews. My campaign was not going unnoticed.

In the Christmas Adjournment debate on 19 December 1983, Mr Peter Shore MP (Lord Shore of Stepney), the late Shadow Leader of the House, in winding up said, 'I hope the Leader of the House will draw the attention of the Minister for Transport to the plea which was made astonishingly expertly by my hon. Friend the Member for Newport East (Mr Hughes).' (Hansard col. 277). In the Easter Adjournment debate on 26 March 1985, the Leader of the House, Mr John Biffen MP (Oswestry), (now Lord Biffen) said, 'The hon. Member for Newport East referred to the Severn Bridge. Year by year as I have sat here, my admiration for the way in which the

Myself with Dai Francis, General Secretary of the South Wales Miners, and Emlyn Williams, President

hon. Gentleman has pursued the issue of the Severn Bridge has grown. One might say that he is the Dalyell of Gwent.' The *South Wales Argus* was now regularly referring to me as Mr Bridge. It was at this time, too, that Mr Speaker Weatherill said that he had always regarded me as the authentic spokesman on the Severn crossing. It was not praise I was looking for but results.

During this period I had one element of criticism from a rather unlikely source. Mr Emlyn Williams, President of the South Wales Miners, said to me, 'Roy, you are spending too much time on the Severn Bridge and not enough on the miners.' In reality I was limited to what I could do for the miners because there were no pits in Newport. Parliamentary protocol was opposed to interference in another Member's constituency and I was always much bothered if anyone interfered in my patch.

Victory, though, was now approaching. On Thursday, 24 July 1986, an announcement was made by Mr Nicholas Edwards MP, Secretary of State for Wales, that plans were being drawn up for a second Severn crossing. In a leading article on Friday 25 July, the *South Wales Argus* stated: 'If one person should be singled out for making this issue his own, it is Newport East MP, Roy Hughes, who has tirelessly chopped away at the might of a Government which had set its face against any such project.' A little later, Mario Basini, (writing in the *Western Mail* (16 February 1987) said, 'When the Government announced its commitment to the second crossing of the Severn estuary last July the collective expression of relief from the Welsh business world was strong enough to rattle the present bridge and its foundations.'

I kept hammering away on the issue of toll charges which I wished to see abolished. Here I was backed up by the Report of the Select Committee on Transport in April 1986, which recommended that tolls should not be imposed on any major estuarial crossings which form part of the motorway or trunk road system and that debts owed to Central Government should be written off immediately and the debts owed to local authority sources should be discharged over a fixed period.

The handsome new bridge was duly opened on 5 June 1996 with a great deal of publicity. As part of the celebrations the bridge had been opened for pedestrians a few days beforehand. Hundreds of people joined in the walk across the bridge from both directions. Many belonged to different groups interested in this new venture. It was a most exhilarating experience – the happiness was infectious. About half way across we met John Cope (MP Northavon, now Lord Cope) who together with many other walkers approached from the Bristol side of the bridge. He presented me with an English rose and I was deeply touched by his gesture.

CHAPTER 14

The Love of My Life

ONE DAY I TOLD Marion that I would like to buy a trench coat, the type worn by Army officers. 'Don't be so daft,' she said.

'Yes,' I said, 'it will be lovely and warm for rugby.' Anyway I went out and bought one and also a checked hat to go with it. Soon it was time to go to Murrayfield and I wore my new outfit. As I went into the stand, the Steward there was dressed exactly as I was. He had a big beaming smile on his face and said, 'Colonel Macleod, I believe – I'm Colonel MacGregor.'

'No,' I said, 'I'm Roy Hughes, Labour Member of Parliament for Newport.' That incident alone, I feel, justified my expenditure on a trench coat.

Soon, though, a dark cloud was to descend on my support for rugby. South Africa has always been a great rugby nation but many people, particularly in my own Party, felt that whilst apartheid prevailed there, all sporting links should be severed. In contrast, the rugby authorities felt that politics should be kept out of sport and over the years they had built up close links with their opposite number, such as Dr Danny Craven in South Africa. Now rugby in Wales has tended to have something of a religious fervour about it. I recall an incident in the House of Commons when Elfed Davies, MP for Rhondda East (Lord Davies of Penrhys), had planned a trip to Scotland for the fixture with Wales. These rugby trips are organised on the basis of a long weekend and Bob Mellish MP (Lord Mellish of Bermondsey) who was then the Labour Chief Whip, tried to stop the errant Member from going. Elfed could be a very determined character and he said to the Chief Whip, 'Bob, you're a Catholic – that is your religion. Rugby is mine and I'm going.' The feeling that prevailed in Wales was that nothing should come in the way of rugby.

Matters came to a head over the apartheid issue when Newport RFC arranged to play the South African Barbarians at Rodney Parade on 27 October 1979. This team was a bit bogus, for it included three or four coloured lads to give the impression of being multi-racial. In fact the coloured contingents, in terms of playing ability, were sub-standard. Opponents of Apartheid tried to prevail on the Club to cancel the fixture but without success. Consequently, on the day of the match there was a large protest march through the town leading to the ground. I had little option but to join in, although I had hoped that wiser counsels would have prevailed, leading to the match being called off. In the event, Newport won the match by twenty-one points to fifteen. The sequel was that a week later the Chairman of Newport RFC asked to come over to see me in my home. When he came his message was that, after a meeting of the Club's committee, a decision had been taken that I was no longer welcome in the Committee box at future matches. He further told me that they could not ban me from the ground. In other words I could still attend fixtures as an ordinary spectator. This I proceeded to do and I stood on the touch line where occasionally constituents would come over to me with a complaint about some problem or other. This period, when I was amongst the crowd and no longer part of the *crachach*, I enjoyed and it gave me an additional opportunity to meet constituents. After about eighteen months I received an invitation to attend the Club's annual dinner, which I accepted, and this was an indication that peace had been restored.

Not long before he died I talked to Wilf Wooller, at a rugby function in Cardiff. In Wales he had been leader of the campaign that politics should not interfere with sport but believed that continuing sporting links was the best way to prevail upon South African leaders to relax the apartheid rules. Wilf now recognised that Nelson Mandela was a great man and he seemed pleased that apartheid had been ended virtually without bloodshed.

I had the good fortune to be present at just about every international in which Wales participated during the glorious seventies. That era produced a host of illustrious players and some of them became household names – Gareth Edwards, Barry John, J.P.R. Williams, Gerald Davies, Phil Bennett. Then there was Merv (The Swerve) Davies, Dai Morris and the legendary Pontypool front row, Faulkener Windsor and Graham Price. Before each home fixture I always attended the Wales Gas Board reception at Snelling House. There present would often be Ambassadors, Cabinet Ministers and occasionally the Prime Minister. Welsh rugby was really on a high! When I asked for my customary gin and tonic, Liz Jenkins, a senior member of the staff who looked after the guests, always insisted that I had a large glass. She soon replaced the small one I was given when I arrived. After the match I went off to the United Services Mess, where I would meet up with old friends from Blackwood. Great days!

Brian Jones, a Newport committee member and former player, advised me, when going to an away fixture, to first contact a director of a Cardiff travel firm. 'Go with them,' he said 'and you can travel with the team.' This I did and as a result I became acquainted with several members of the WRU and individual players. Cliff Jones became a real friend and at this time he was Chairman of Selectors. A native of the Rhondda, he had been a brilliant outside half in the thirties for Cambridge University, Cardiff and Wales. It was appropriate, I thought, that in the centenary year of the WRU he was made President.

On 4 February 1978 Wales beat Ireland in Dublin to record a third triple Crown victory in succession. Coming home on the plane the following day, Jack Young, a member of the WRU from West Wales who later became President said to me, 'Roy, when you get back you must do something for these boys.'

'Jack' I said, 'I promise.' On Monday, back in Westminster, I approached John Morris, the Secretary of State for Wales, with the suggestion that something should be done for the Welsh Rugby team to mark their success. He in turn approached the Prime Minister, James Callaghan, and so on Monday, 3 April 1978, a reception was held at Number Ten for the team, members of the WRU and certain Welsh MPs who were interested in rugby. The Prime Minister when welcoming the guests said that he had recently met the President of the USA but, turning to the President of the WRU (T. Rowley Jones, Deputy Head of Brynmawr Comprehensive School), he said, 'But you are the real President.' The reception concluded with the singing of 'Mae Haen Wlad Fy Nhadau' and there to lead the singing was none other than Sir Geraint Evans. What an evening!

In more recent years and since he entered the House of Commons in 1987, I have been friendly with Paul Murphy (the Member for Torfaen) and now the Secretary of State for Northern Ireland. Together with his father Ron and sometimes his brother Neil we went a number of times to internationals, both in Dublin and Paris. Ron could never forget his Irish roots and always wore a green scarf when Wales played Ireland. By now the playing record of the Welsh team had deteriorated somewhat but this was counterbalanced by the warmth of the hospitality we received. On one occasion I went to Scotland with a party from Caldicot which was in my constituency. With Dylan Thomas in mind, they called themselves Llareggub RFC, having never lost a match because they never played one. The name of the Club seemed so definitely Welsh and so

With Rt. Hon. Paul Murphy, Secretary of State for Northern Ireland.

much less spelt backwards. I had had a pretty tough week in
Westminster but I thought I would at least be able to get my
head down on the coach. This I proceeded to do but was
quickly awakened by the exclamation, 'No sleeping on tour.' It
is a hard life being a rugby supporter.

In 1997 I became President of the Newport Athletic Club
which had been formed in 1875. It catered for a host of sports
but rugby football was always predominant. The hallmark of
the Club was the amateur ethic, with a host of voluntary
workers. In his letter inviting me to become President, the
Honorary Secretary, Campbell Black, wished me 'a long and
successful term of office'. Alas, it was not to be, for the
professional era was looming. The changeover was quite
dramatic for soon a company was formed to run the rugby club
with a small Board of Directors. Newport has been fortunate
in having the valuable support of Mr Tony Brown who holds
the position of Chief Executive. He owns the Bisley Company

which makes office furniture and its factory in Newport employs several hundred people. Through his good offices large sums of money have been put into the Club, thus enabling it to bring in star players largely from overseas. For twenty years or so Newport had been referred to as a sleeping giant but it is resurgent once again, well equipped and able to take on the best in Europe.

Over the years due to Parliamentary and constituency business, I was never able to go abroad on a Lions tour. This is when a squad of players is selected, drawn from each of the four home rugby unions. In 2001 the tour was to Australia and I was determined to go. In the first test in Brisbane it was fascinating to hear the singing. 'Cockles and Mussels' from Ireland, 'Flower of Scotland', 'Sweet Chariot', and from Wales came the familiar 'Cwm Rhondda'.

Twenty-two year old Johnny Wilkinson, the England and Lions outside half from Newcastle, said that during this first test, when he heard the resounding tones of 'Cwm Rhondda', he felt a tingling at the back of his neck. The old revivalist hymn had been sung with great gusto by the huge Welsh contingent, which was by far the largest touring party.

For the second test at Melbourne, the Australian Rugby Union took a decision to close the roof of the stadium and this was the first time that I and thousands of other rugby supporters had ever witnessed a rugby match in an enclosed area. The preliminary proceedings were turned into something like a 'Pop' concert and the deafening noise affected one's ear drums. Here I speculated that this was a means of drowning out the singing and cheering from the large contingent of Lions supporters, which had been such a feature of the Brisbane fixture. There was also a report a day or two before the game that the Australian RFU had allocated £80,000 to ensure that their supporters were properly kitted out in order to match the sea of red of their opponents' supporters. When there was a stoppage during the course of the match a series of messages was broadcast over the tannoy. Spectators were warned that if they transgressed on to the playing pitch they could be fined so many dollars. A similar rather authoritarian message came over regarding the 'No Smoking' rule. Annoyance was compounded when from time to time a commercial advertisement was broadcast to thank major sponsors for their support. I felt these proceedings were in rather poor taste. I was further irritated when the Lions lost the match after their first half superiority and scoring opportunities. The final showdown in Sydney was a touch-and-go affair. It could have gone either way and the result was not finally decided until the closing stages. In the event Australia won and probably narrowly deserved to do so. People in Australia were most friendly and welcoming. It is a young vibrant country, but I formed the impression that in sporting activities they do not like to lose.

CHAPTER 15

Callaghan's Premiership

FOLLOWING THE OCTOBER 1974 General Election Harold
Wilson became Prime Minister for the fourth time,
equalling the record of Gladstone, and he was only fifty-eight
years of age. Nevertheless, what many did not know or
appreciate was that he was already planning his retirement.
Enoch Powell had a famous saying that 'all political lives unless
they are cut off in mid-stream at a happy juncture end in
failure because that is the nature of human affairs.' Wilson,
however, wanted an orderly retirement, as if he were a bank
manager or a headmaster, and I feel there was nothing
underhand about his plans. He would retire to an academic life
and this would please Mary who was never happy when
engaging in public life. There was, however, unfinished
business in the form of a referendum on the Common Market
that had been promised in the manifesto for the October 1974
General Election. The Prime Minister was now determined to
stay in, but here he was in opposition to his own Party and
some of his Cabinet colleagues. He was never very pro-Europe
but believed that, if we pulled out, Jenkins and his colleagues
would leave the Party, whereas the Anti Marketeers – Shore,
Silkin and Benn – had nowhere to go. His judgement in
retrospect, though, can be questioned because before too long
the so-called 'Gang of Four' would break with Labour to form
a new Social Democratic Party.

In the event he was clever enough to win the argument
whilst avoiding splitting the Labour Movement and at the
same time settling the argument over membership of the

European Community for years to come. He should never have been allowed to get away with it because a special Party Conference held in London on 26 April 1975, voted two to one in favour of coming out. The 'Yes' vote was won in the referendum on 5 June 1975 when sixty-seven per cent of the electorate voted to stay in the Common Market.

With this major issue settled it was now the economy that needed his full attention. Prices were rising fast and the Chancellor of the Exchequer, Dennis Healey, was calling for a statutory incomes policy. Such a policy was anathema to the trades unions, as well as being ruled out by a manifesto commitment. In the event a voluntary approach was decided upon and, on 2 July 1975, the Prime Minister agreed with Jack Jones, General Secretary of the T&GWU, a limit of a six pound increase in wages for all workers. The Labour Government was fortunate at this stage in that leading their respective Unions were two outstanding figures, Hugh Scanlon and Jack Jones. They were both conscious of the wider picture and fearful of another 1931 situation, which had rocked the Labour Movement from top to bottom and led to the downfall of the Labour Government. Its Prime Minister, Ramsay MacDonald, proceeded to lead a Tory-dominated Coalition Government.

Wilson had another local difficulty through what he considered to be the intransigence of Tony Benn. Following his October victory, the Prime Minister got tough and insisted that Benn accepted Cabinet collective responsibility. Benn was forced to comply and was dealt a further blow when Wilson moved him from Trade and Industry to Energy. He contemplated resignation but was prevailed on to stay in the Cabinet.

Wilson ultimately was true to himself and retired at sixty. His decision, however, provoked all manner of lurid theories. It was suggested that he was being hounded by the Secret

Service, blackmailed or that there was tension between him and members of his staff. Personally, I feel all these theories can be dismissed and what made him reach this decision was his state of health. I seem to recall that he had a very serious operation when he was Leader of HM Opposition during the period of the Heath Government. Perhaps, too, he became conscious of the fact that his mind and phenomenal memory had started to deteriorate. Later, of course, he was struck with Alzheimers disease. I recall, after he had left office, seeing him walking around the corridors of the Commons a lonely man. So many to whom he had done favours just did not want to know him. In those days I used to talk to him a bit because frankly I always had a soft spot for him. I also recall happier days when he regularly came to chat at the Welsh table in the tearoom of the House of Commons.

In the leadership contest that followed Wilson's resignation, James Callaghan defeated Michael Foot by 176 votes to 137. The Callaghan premiership was to last for three years and one month and for more than half this period the Government could claim success from an economic and political standpoint. Jim Callaghan, 'Sunny Jim' as he became known, was popular in the country and he performed well in the House of Commons. By contrast the Leader of HM Opposition, Margaret Thatcher, seemed to lack lustre and the Prime Minister invariably got the better of the exchanges when they argued on the floor of the Chamber. The parlous Party situation regarding votes was remedied by the Lib/Lab pact and Callaghan got on well with the young leader of the Liberals, David Steel, who had succeeded Jeremy Thorpe.

Another important landmark and a boost to confidence was when Chancellor Dennis Healey announced that Britain would be self-sufficient in oil by 1980. People like Jack Jones were keen that oil revenues should be utilised to revitalise and expand our manufacturing industry through major new investment. This point of view was overruled and the new revenues were absorbed into the Treasury coffers. Our older industrial regions like South Wales and the North of England, where unemployment is endemic, would be in a far more prosperous position today had Jack Jones' advice been heeded. At this time Jack was at the height of his power and was sometimes referred to in the media as 'Emperor Jones'. What I can say is that whatever power he achieved he always used it in a most responsible manner. One day I went to meet him to take him up to a Committee Room in the Commons, where he was to speak on 'Ports and their importance to the British economy'. As we walked along the corridors, no fewer than three Secretaries of State came up to him to pay homage, so to speak. To me, this was a measure of the respect in which he was held.

Labour had been committed to devolution for Scotland and Wales but this proved to be a contentious issue in the ranks of the Parliamentary Labour Party when the legislation came up for debate in Parliament. I was naturally interested in the Welsh aspect of the discussions that were taking place. There were endless exchanges of opinion in the Welsh Labour Group and at one stage we were meeting almost daily to try and reach an agreed stand. Eventually this was achieved, so I was rather surprised that later Neil Kinnock toured the country in opposition to the Labour Government's proposals. This, too, after he stated in two consecutive General Elections that a future Labour Government would bring devolution to Scotland and Wales. He was backed up by Leo Abse MP (Pontypool), whose opposition was rather more of an emotional and anti-nationalist character. Personally I spoke at numerous meetings throughout the country in favour of the Government's proposals but I sensed very early on that there was little popular support. Resistance to the Government's proposals also came from the County Councils who felt that an elected assembly sitting in Cardiff would undermine their position. In the event their survival was shortlived for they were abolished by a total reorganisation of local government brought about by the Conservatives in their Local Government (Wales) Act 1994, which replaced the twelve Counties and thirty-seven Districts in Wales with twenty-two Unitary Authorities. These changes came into effect in April 1995.

The first meeting at which I spoke was in my home village of Pontllanfraith and there they were still reeling from the heavy price they were paying in Council rates due to the abominable reorganisation of local government carried out by the Tory Government in 1972/73. This reorganisation cost the earth and, at the end of it, I would say we probably had a worse form of local government than we had hitherto. I could understand the attitude of the people of Pontllanfraith, for they felt that they would be faced with the additional financial burden of a Welsh Assembly. In fact this was a misguided point of view because the new proposed legislative arrangements were to be financed directly from the Treasury. The situation was not helped by the luke-warm attitude of the Prime Minister to the proposals of the Government of which he was the head. I felt, too, that his attitude had percolated down to certain other Ministers.

Jim Callaghan was the principal speaker at a Pro-Devolution Rally in Swansea on 21 February 1979 but I felt it was a lack-lustre performance. Some commentators took the view that he was not in favour of devolution but merely using the issue to buy time for his minority Government. As Kenneth Morgan wrote in his official biography of Callaghan: 'He ploughed the sands of Celtic devolution in the latter 1970s without enthusiasm or great commitment.'[*] In the referendum vote the Government's proposals were heavily defeated. The

---

[*]*Callaghan – A Life.* p. 510.

Secretary of State for Wales, John Morris QC, was a fervent devolutionist but as he put it 'You have to recognise a pink elephant when you find it on your doorstep.' There was some solace to my ego a little later when Ron Evans, Michael Foot's agent in the Ebbw Vale constituency, told me that Michael said that I had justified my place in the Commons if only for the work I had done over devolution.

James Callaghan had a 'thing' about Education, particularly stemming from the fact that he never went to University. In fact he was in good company, for the two celebrated Prime Ministers of the twentieth century, namely Winston Churchill and David Lloyd George, were similarly disadvantaged. Despite colossal sums of money being spent on Education, standards of performance in our schools seemed to be falling. Callaghan was very concerned and he resolved to put the spotlight on the issue. The venue chosen for his pronouncement was Ruskin College, Oxford, in October 1976. It was my old college and I was invited to the gathering. Despite the depth of his feeling and his sincerity, his reception by the students was far from welcoming, for they chanted and jeered at him. At the end of the meeting they sang 'The Red Flag' but then they struck out with the opening words of the 'Internationale' – 'Arise ye starvelings from your slumbers...' The singing began to peter out and Jim was quick to intervene saying, 'Ah, you don't know the words.' This was a kind of dig at their socialist pretensions. He was quite right, too, in calling for Labour to adopt a less doctrinaire approach towards state schools and expressing the need for high professional standards and quality control. Citizens should be aware of rights and duties and social obligations to others.

An incident in which I was involved related to a pay dispute at the Ford Motor Company. The company had made huge profits and I felt quite rightly that the workers deserved their share, for otherwise the money would simply be shipped back

to America. This was the point of view put forward by Moss
Evans who by now had succeeded Jack Jones as General
Secretary of the T&GWU. The claim of the Union had greater
credence because the Chairman of Ford, Terry Beckett, had
awarded himself an increase of eighty per cent. There was a
seven week strike and the Ford workers eventually returned to
work after settling for a wage increase of around seventeen per
cent.

Financial sanctions were now to be imposed by the
Government on the Ford Motor Company, for the settlement
they had reached with the Unions was far above the Government's five per cent norm. First, however, Parliamentary
approval had to be obtained and a handful of us stayed out of
the division lobbies refusing to vote for the Government,
which was defeated by 285 votes to 279. I found it illogical to
support a workers' pay claim and then to vote for sanctions
against the Company which made a deal with Unions. It was a
traumatic occasion, for Ian Mikardo for one was urging me to
vote with the Government. Likewise, my close friend the
Stoke-on-Trent MP Bob Cant actually tried to pull me into the
lobby. The following day when the Prime Minister James
Callaghan moved a vote of confidence, I and other rebels
returned to the fold and the Government was successful by
300 votes to 290.

James Callaghan was expected to call a General Election in
September 1978 and many people were amazed when, at the
TUC Conference, he sang a verse of the song 'Waiting at the
Church.' In opting to carry on he made a fundamental mistake,
though a number of senior colleagues at the time tended to
agree with his decision, including Michael Foot and the Chief
Whip, Michael Cocks. However, industrial turmoil was
looming and the Government was eventually faced with what
became known as the 'Winter of Discontent'.

In March 1979, in a censure vote in the Commons, the

Government was defeated by one vote. The Liberals and the Scottish Nationalists voted with the Tories, as did eight Ulster Unionists. Callaghan was dignified in defeat and straight away called upon HM the Queen to dissolve Parliament. The General Election was held on Thursday 3 May and the Conservatives had a clear majority of forty-four seats.

In Newport we held our own, the results being as follows:

R.J. Hughes (Lab)	30,919
Gerald Davies (Con)	21,742
A. Lambert (Lib)	6,270
A. Vickery (Plaid Cymru)	473
Mrs G. Woodhouse (National Front)	454
Labour majority	9,177

CHAPTER 16

The Thatcher Years

Lord, make me an instrument of your peace.
Where there is hatred, let me sow love;
Where there is injury, pardon;
Where there is doubt, faith;
Where there is despair, hope;
Where there is darkness, light
Where there is sadness, joy.

IT WAS 1979 and thus the prayer of St Francis of Assisi spoken from the steps of Number Ten Downing Street began the dark night of Thatcherism. Over the years what happened in practice was a complete repudiation of the noble sentiments expressed in the prayer.

Margaret Thatcher had been Leader of the Conservative Party since 1975 and was now in office as Prime Minister for eleven and a half years. I must say it seemed like an eternity. As soon as she stepped into Cabinet office, it became clear that she intended to put her own stamp on all future initiatives. In doing so she changed the British political scene beyond all recognition.

She was first determined to destroy the power and influence of the trade unions and various Acts of Parliament were put through to help bring this about. Such initiatives were gleefully welcomed by the right wing but also supported by large sections of the press. At the time, as I recall, the attempt was made, not without success, to give ordinary working people the impression that the trade unions were their enemy.

In post-war years, the British people had grown accustomed to an economy run on the basis of full employment, or something close to it. With the election of the new Thatcher Government, with its free market, non-interference policies, unemployment began to soar and in 1981 reached three million, a figure described by the Prime Minister as 'alarming'. The difficulties were compounded by high interest rates.

A major new development came in April 1982 when the Argentinians captured Fort Stanley in the Falklands and Michael Foot, by now Leader of the Labour Party, gave Margaret Thatcher full backing in the war that followed. Michael's stance, although well-intentioned, was not over-whelmingly received in the ranks of the Parliamentary Labour Party or in the Party in the country. The Government was not particularly popular at the time but it was the jingoism engendered by the Falklands war, together with the creation of the SDP, that led to the Thatcher victory in May 1983. The Tories increased their majority with 397 seats to Labour's 209 and the Alliance's 23. The so-called 'Gang of Four', Roy Jenkins, David Owen, Bill Rogers and Shirley Williams had broken away to form their own Party. To my mind this was treachery of the highest order. I recall that throughout the election campaign in Newport, a Labour political defector with rather a tarnished background stood outside our Party office holding aloft an SDP banner. The SDP had undoubtedly undermined Labour, which had forty-nine fewer seats than in any post-war election, its share of votes falling to 27.6 per cent. The new Alliance of SDP and Liberals received 25.5 per cent which put Labour in its worst electoral position since 1931. The greatest bugbear I found in Newport was our anti-nuclear policy, for at every other door we knocked on this issue was raised. People had rather a Dunkirk attitude, i.e. if the enemy had tanks, we should, too. They reasoned, therefore, that the same yardstick should apply in regard to nuclear weapons.

There is one part of Alway Ward which has rather a large concentration of unmarried mothers and one day I was on the street handing out Party literature when along came a young lady with a baby in the pram and a toddler by her side. I thought to myself 'She will vote for us' so I asked her politely to support our cause. She replied 'I will not be voting Labour because I do not like your Defence policy.' That brief interview and the response have stayed in my mind ever since.

What was rather irritating during the election campaign was that in Newport town centre on 25 May, Jim Callaghan openly attacked his own Party's policies. 'Our refusal to give up arms unilaterally had brought better and more realistic proposals from the Soviet Union and the West should not dismantle their weapons for nothing in return.' Jim Callaghan has spent a lifetime lecturing Party workers on the need for loyalty but on this occasion he was the transgressor. Yet, from my own experience of knocking on doors in Newport during the campaign, our official policy of unilateral disarmament was anathema to the electors.

I recall a conversation I had around this time, one morning at the Labour Party Conference in Blackpool, with Arthur Scargill shortly, I believe, before he became President of the National Union of Mineworkers. He knew I was a Member of Parliament and almost immediately he began to give his views on the difference between industrial and political leadership and the relative significance, in his view, of the former. A person reaching even the rank of Cabinet Minister is manipulated by civil servants and on leaving office is quickly forgotten. By comparison, a leading trade unionist is his own man, so to speak, far more able to make an impression and with a likelihood of a niche in the history books. I trust I am not misrepresenting Arthur Scargill's point of view but I have often thought of that conversation bearing in mind subsequent events in the mining industry.

One of Margaret Thatcher's early measures was an announcement that some of the coalmines were to be closed. This caused great bitterness in the industry and on 6 March 1984 the miners began their great strike which lasted for twelve months. Earlier, the Government had been forced to retreat before the miners' demands on wages and in their opposition to pit closures, but this time they were ready for the challenge. Coal had been stockpiled and some coal-fired power stations had been converted to oil. Ian MacGregor, a former Chairman of the British Steel Corporation, had earlier been transferred to the Chairmanship of the National Coal Board. He was regarded as a hard man.

For some years I had been Chairman of the Steel Group of Labour MPs and in this capacity I had got to know Ian MacGregor a little. He was a Scot by birth but during the Second World War had taken up a position in America involving atomic energy. Apparently any person involved in that sensitive area had to be an American citizen. I noted he was always keen to come across to the House of Commons to speak to our members and was rather lavish, I thought, with hospitality.

A major secret weapon of the Government was the Nottinghamshire miners who refused to join the strike and continued working throughout the year long dispute. This area of the coalfield has had a long history of collaboration with employers. 'Spencerism', or the 'scab' union as it became known, originated from Nottingham and the members did everything possible to undermine the South Wales miners in the disputes of the late 1920s and 30s. Their behaviour is etched in the memory of the older miners. For me their stand in 1984-85 was merely a case of history repeating itself. This time they called themselves the Union of Democratic Mine-workers and collaborated wholeheartedly with the Thatcher Government. From the outset the police were heavily involved and the Home Secretary, Leon Brittan, made clear that they had the power to turn pickets back and to disperse them if they assembled in excessive numbers. With the exception of the Metropolitan Police, he had no direct power over them for Great Britain had no national police force. To overcome this difficulty the National Reporting Centre was activated in Scotland Yard, allowing the police to pool intelligence and to co-ordinate assistance from one force to another.

Arthur Scargill had to some extent played into the hands of the Government by publicly stating after the Conservative General Election victory in 1983, that 'he did not accept that we are landed for the next four years with this Government'. In putting forward this point of view, he seems to have been influenced by the document 'The Miners' Next Step' which came out as a result of the formation of an unofficial Reform Committee way back in 1922 and which was intended to instil into the leadership of the South Wales miners and the Parliamentary leaders a more militant spirit. It was essentially a syndicalist concept and as James Connelly, the Irish leader, put it 'they who rule industrially will rule politically'. One of the authors of the document was Noah Abblet, who is thought to have considerably influenced Aneurin Bevan, Arthur Horner and other miners' leaders in their early days. Abblet put the case against the roundabout method of acting through Parliament in the simple question, 'Why cross the river to fill the pail?' At the time such a theory looked immensely formidable when Labour was so much stronger in the coalfield than at Westminster. For me personally, a repudiation of this path forward came with the election of the Labour Government in 1945 and its overwhelming majority. In 1949 the adoption meeting for Harold Finch as the Parliamentary Labour candidate for the Bedwellty constituency took place in the Miners' Institute, Blackwood. Supporting his nomination was James Griffiths, then Minister for National Insurance, who was a former President of the South Wales Miners. He contrasted the gains for ordinary people as a result of the election of the Attlee Government and as he put it 'so painlessly obtained'. By comparison, earlier industrial action had resulted in loss of wages, debt and in some instances families facing starvation.

Margaret Thatcher in turn described the miners as 'the enemy within', which I felt was an offence. Miners are unique, for the arduous and hazardous nature of their work made them so. Likewise, miners' wives appreciated the dangers involved and this in turn helped to build a spirit of trust and co-operation so markedly reflected in the mining localities. They have not been referred to for nothing as the 'Brigade of Guards' of the Labour Movement

Harold MacMillan, the former Conservative Prime Minister, following his elevation to the House of Lords as the Earl of Stockton, in his maiden speech on 13 November 1984 said:

'Although at my age I cannot interfere or do anything about it, it breaks my heart to see what is happening in our country today. A terrible strike is being carried on by the best men in the world. They beat the Kaiser's army and they beat Hitler's army. They never gave in. The strike is pointless and endless. We cannot afford action of this kind.'

The miners' strike dragged on but in July 1984 talks began between the National Coal Board and the miners' leaders. Things were beginning to look hopeful, for the employers were now putting forward the proposal that 'no pit should be closed if it was capable of being beneficially developed'. They were also prepared to give a commitment to keep open five named pits which the NUM had claimed were due for closure.

It was at this stage that Margaret Thatcher truly showed her hand. In her book *The Downing Street Years* (pages 357-8) she points out 'We were very alarmed', believing that such a settlement would have given Arthur Scargill the chance to claim victory. She goes on to say that 'on 18 July negotiations collapsed. I have to say I was enormously relieved.' This was the same lady who, when she was first installed as Prime Minister, espoused the peaceful homilies of St Francis!

Throughout the stoppage I found little hostility towards the miners and their cause. On the contrary they were showered with gifts and financial donations. Depots were set up around the country as collection points for what people had to offer, such as groceries and clothes. My daughters recall attending a special fund-raising concert in London, where there were standing ovations and tears. Labour MPs were making financial donations.

Early in November 1984 Indira Gandhi, the Indian Prime Minister, was assassinated by one of her bodyguards and Neil Kinnock, as Leader, was deputed to represent the Labour Party at her funeral. Coinciding with this was the Annual Chartist rally in his constituency which he was due to chair and he phoned me in the Commons asking if I would stand in for him. This I was only too pleased to do, for it gave me an opportunity to identify with the miners and their struggle. Newport, which I represented in Parliament, had no pits and over the years it has concentrated on steel production. We had a full house in the Leisure Centre at my old school in Pontllanfraith. Michael Meacher MP, at present Minister for the Environment, was the guest speaker and representatives of miners' wives also spoke. The atmosphere was full of fervour and support for the strike. From all reports it would seem I did rather well as Chairman. Mrs Willis, besides being Neil Kinnock's Secretary, was the wife of Norman Willis, General Secretary of the TUC, and she was full of praise.

The South Wales coalfield remained solid but weakness began to show in some other areas. In North Derbyshire, for example, there was a move towards getting back to work and at this time the NCB took the initiative by announcing that miners who were back in work by Monday 19 November, would qualify for a substantial Christmas bonus. Peter Walker, the Energy Secretary, issued a statement to the effect that he had been informed by the Chairman of the Central Electricity Generating Board that the level of coal production that had now been achieved was such that there would be no power cuts during the whole of 1985. By the end of February more than half of the members of the NUM were not on strike. On Sunday 3 March an NUM Delegates' Conference voted for a return to work after the strike had lasted a full twelve months.

It was a defeat on a major scale, not only for the miners but the whole of the Labour Movement. Before very long the coal mining industry in Britain was wrecked. In South Wales every pit was closed, with the exception of Tower Colliery in Hirwaun which is worker-owned and has been a success story.

Going back to the days of the 1945 Labour Government, a huge programme of public ownership was put into effect. Great state monopolies were created along the lines advocated by Herbert Morrison. They tended to be bureaucratic and insensitive. It would have been wiser to have organised in smaller, more localised units and with the workers more involved in management.

For South Wales the closure of the coalfield meant the end of an era. I look now with sadness at the dereliction and deprivation in many of our valley towns. We had coal in abundance and to my mind it is such a valuable product. Some people say it is good that all the pits are closed, believing that the life of a miner was such an inhuman existence. They are probably right. Nevertheless, from reports in the media there is now speculation about an energy shortage in the years ahead.

Other sweeping changes were brought about. Many public utilities such as water, electricity, gas and local transport were taken over by the private sector and support services for education and the NHS (e.g. catering and cleaning) were also put out to tender.

Another drastic change which I must say altered our perspectives was the sale of Council houses to sitting tenants – the longer the tenancy, the cheaper the house. Naturally it was an unpopular measure with Labour who could only stand aghast on the side-lines, so to speak, while the policy went ahead. This was an issue in the 1983 election campaign, because it was rumoured that if Labour won the election the policy would be scrapped and houses which had been sold would be returned to the local Councils. The rumour was without foundation. With hindsight, it could be regarded as a good policy and over the years it has had a marked effect on Council housing. As the new owners took full responsibility for their properties, their pride was visible in their gardens and their new front door. From this angle it could be said that Council housing reached its full potential.

The following years were difficult ones for Margaret Thatcher. Unemployment was still high at three million and the opinion polls showed a steady increase in support for Labour. I think voters were becoming rather irritated by her confrontational autocratic style. One of her big problems arose in 1985. A smallish West country helicopter company, Westland, was in financial trouble and the question arose as to whether they should look to an American investment by the Sikorski Company of some 29.3 per cent, which would in effect give them control of Westland, or whether they should look towards Europe for future Defence orders. Heseltine, then Minister of Defence and a fervent European, believed our destiny was closely linked with Western Europe. The whole issue became an entanglement and on 9 January he resigned his post by walking out of a Cabinet meeting. Michael Heseltine was a powerful figure in Government and Thatcher felt the blow keenly.

Others were to follow. Nigel Lawson, Chancellor of the Exchequer, resigned in October 1989 following disagreement with Thatcher who was unwilling to join the ERM (Exchange Rate Mechanism) and a year later Geoffrey Howe, Foreign Secretary and a keen supporter of European monetary union, became so angered by her intransigent opposition to the issue that he resigned in November 1990. Nicholas Ridley (Environment) had resigned earlier.

John Major succeeded Nigel Lawson as Chancellor of the Exchequer in 1989. At that time inflation was running high, often into double figures, while interest rates were unacceptably high. He was of the opinion that our best course of action would be to join the ERM in order to stabilise the pound sterling. Thatcher was less than enthusiastic about it and it was with reluctance that she went along with joining. We remained in it for two years and a certain amount of acrimony was caused when we actually left. John Major, in his autobiography indicated that 'no one held a pistol to Margaret's head, and the suggestion that this formidable woman was a pushover in the hands of her new Chancellor was unreal. It was sufficient to say that we entered the ERM to general applause and left it with general abuse.' The Prime Minister's difficulties were compounded by the so-called Poll Tax, which was introduced in 1990-91. This was a tax which replaced Council rates by a tax on individuals. It had already been put in place the previous year in Scotland – in a way Scotland was the guinea pig. It was unpopular there. The new tax was then brought into action in the remainder of Britain but it generated so much anger, as demonstrated throughout the country, that it had to be abandoned after one year and the old system of Council rates was re-established. The poll tax was seen as a disastrous and expensive experiment. These troubles caused much anxiety amongst Tory MPs, especially those who held marginal seats. As the Government had such a large majority, it seemed likely that many would be affected. And so began the process which saw the fall of Thatcher. The mounting disquiet was such that she faced the inevitable and entered the contest. Her opponent was Michael Heseltine. She had a majority of votes but not quite enough to secure her success. After much deliberation and consultation with colleagues, she decided to withdraw from the contest. At this stage other contenders entered the ring and the outcome was that John Major was elected.

CHAPTER 17

After Thatcher

JOHN MAJOR WAS Prime Minister from 1992 to 1997. His term of office was not as turbulent as Thatcher's which was bedevilled by problems with the EEC and which split the Government in half. The country was in recession in the years 1990-93 and a decision was made to join the ERM in 1990 which in effect anchored the pound sterling to the Deutschmark. International pressures on the German currency had made its value soar, while the pound sterling plummeted to an unsustainable level. Membership of the ERM was suspended in 1992. Another EEC problem facing Major was the Maastricht Treaty, which laid out measures for a common currency among member states. Public opinion in Britain was against such a move and so Major secured an 'opt-out' agreement in 1993.

Neil Kinnock as Leader of the Labour Party since 1983 had seen over the years a gradual recovery of Labour and he undoubtedly laid the foundations of the success that was to follow. When the next General Election was held in 1992, success was well within our reach. Indeed the opinion polls gave us a lead of a few points. Labour was shattered by the results of the election. The Tories had 336 seats, Labour 271, the Liberal Democrats twenty and the Scottish and Welsh Nationalist Parties seven between them. In Newport East I had a majority of 9,899.

At this time Neil resigned as Leader of the Labour Party and John Smith MP (Monklands East) was elected in his place. John was a man of formidable intellect and integrity. Canny.

His untimely death two years later came as a great shock to everyone. I recall attending a service in Llandaff Cathedral where a large TV screen enabled us to share in the funeral service in Scotland. We were stunned, hardly believing what was being shown.

John Major wrote generously of him – 'He had no malice. There were things that he cared for passionately. He lived for them, he fought for them, he cared for them. But he carried his fight fairly, without malice, without nastiness . . . When I think of John Smith, I think of an opponent, not an enemy, and when I remember him, I shall do so with respect and affection.'

Major will be remembered for the privatisation of the railways in 1993. It proved disastrous, all the more so because the railway system was fragmented into component parts which were sold off separately. The failures of the system were bequeathed to the subsequent Labour Government.

The Major years will also be remembered for 'sleaze', which marred the image of the Government. Neil Hamilton and Tim Smith, both Ministers, admitted under pressure that they had taken cash and other benefits from Mohammed Al Fayed in return for putting down Parliamentary Questions. Neither Hamilton nor Smith had recorded these interests in the Register of Interests, as they were required to do. It is true that these incidents occurred before Major became Prime Minister, but they did 'stick'. Three other cases came to light – Piers Merchant MP and Alan Stewart MP, together with Micky Hirst, Chairman of the Tory Party in Scotland, all caused embarrassment to Major when details of their private lives were revealed by the press. The Tories had been in Government for some eighteen years and now the writing was on the wall. The feeling throughout the country was that they had run their course. John Major himself said, 'The opinion polls were so bad that we had little reason to expect victory.'

*With the Mayor of Newport, Councillor Ken Powell, and Mayoress;
Councillor Mrs Joan Jepps; Mr Les Jepps; Councillor and Mrs Ron
Morris, Deputy Mayor and Mayoress, visiting our home in Abergavenny.*

Following the death of John Smith the new Leader of the
Labour Party was Tony Blair, MP for Sedgefield. He was a man
of extraordinary vision. Over the long years of Toryism, the
country had changed drastically, both socially and economically
– so much so that there was no going back. The only way was
to go forward and this he masterminded with New Labour. It
had a wide-ranging appeal throughout the country. Its scope
was so extensive that the Opposition parties were squeezed
into a corner and left with little room for manoeuvre. I
remember vividly the evening of Election Day – May Day
1997. The results coming through on the TV were so
astounding* that we were reluctant to go to bed. Finally at
4.30 a.m. we made our way upstairs.

A new day was dawning.

*Labour majority – 199.

CHAPTER 18

The House of Lords

As a family we had always had a 'yen' for Abergavenny and in 1990 we were fortunate to be able to move there. Abergavenny is a peaceful yet vibrant market town, nestling in an area surrounded by seven hills. One of the hills, Ysgyryd Fawr,* has an awe-inspiring appearance. It is as if a giant had stood on the summit and angrily split it with an axe. There is a local legend that this hill was torn in two on the day of the Crucifixion and so it is called the Holy Mountain. It is customary for Churchgoers in the neighbourhood to join together and climb the mountain on Good Friday. The weekly market is a big attraction to visitors and no doubt inspired the song-writer – 'Take a Trip to Abergavenny'.

Soon afterwards I began to look to the future. There is no doubt that Members of Parliament work very hard indeed and the pressures are formidable. The constant travelling between London and the constituency, the long working hours in Westminster, often unpredictable, all take their toll. After a week's work in London, the weekends are occupied with engagements in the constituency and regular surgeries which result in considerable correspondence.

One other factor – MPs are very much aware that they are in the public eye all the time and can seldom feel 'switched off'. In this connection I recall a story told by a colleague, Tom Williams, who had a Welsh background and was a Baptist Minister before going to the Commons. He was in hospital

---

*Skirrid Fawr.

Family photograph on my introduction to the House of Lords, 1997.

after surgery and was just struggling back to consciousness, when he became aware of a fellow patient at his bedside who said, 'I'm told you are an MP. Could you take up a problem for me?'

I had already been re-selected for the forthcoming General Election but after considerable thought decided to resign my seat. One of the candidates was Alan Howarth, a former Conservative MP for Stratford-on-Avon, who had joined the Labour Party on disillusionment with the Tories. We attended the selection conference as observers. Naturally we had mixed feelings and old memories came crowding in. Alan won the contest with a large majority. Not long afterwards, Tony Blair sent for me and told me he was sending me to the Lords.

Many formalities had to be gone through and one thing that had to be decided upon was my new title. As it happened the name Hughes was the most common in Westminster and over the years much confusion had arisen. It was suggested that I changed my name, so I chose Islwyn, which is the name of a mountain overlooking my old home (Mynyddislwyn). It was also the bardic title of a local poet, William Thomas, who was well known in the area around the middle of the nineteenth century. Of course Newport was included in the title so I became Lord Islwyn of Casnewydd in the County of Gwent.

My formal introduction into the Lords took place in November 1997 and I was one of the last to take part in the full historic ceremony which was shortly afterwards streamlined. It was a memorable gathering of relatives and close friends, although we were restricted in numbers. Among the guests were my good friend and neighbour John Williams and his wife Kay, while Marion was delighted to welcome her old Convent School friend Doreen Lakin and her husband Ken.

Among the many congratulations I received was one I particularly valued – a most unusual one. Our youngest daughter, Meriel, is a skilled bellringer, who had once rung in

Westminster Abbey ('shaking like a leaf'). She presented me with this picture:

The Derby Diocesan Association of Church Bell Ringers

**At St Lawrence's Church, Long Eaton, Derbyshire,
On Thursday November 6th., 1997, in 2 hours 26 minutes,**

A Peal of 5040 Surprise Minor in 7 Methods:
London, Bourne, Ipswich, Norwich, Beverley, Surfleet, Cambridge

Tenor 6 cwt. 2 qr. 6 lb. in B flat

Treble Brian A. Tomlinson
2   John A. Cater
3   The Hon. Meriel A. Hughes
4   Alistair E. Smith
5   S. Clarke Walters
Tenor John E. Heaton

Conducted by John E. Heaton

Rung to celebrate the elevation to the peerage of Roy Hughes, now Lord Islwyn of Casnewydd, father of the ringer of the third.

I soon adapted to the new life. I find working in the Lords less confrontational than in the Commons and many of the old pressures are gone. The volume of work, however, is still considerable but there is a quiet ambience about the place. It is generally assumed that the Labour Government in power has control over the Lords but in fact the percentage of Labour Peers is only twenty-nine. It becomes increasingly difficult to get our legislation through and Baroness 'Josie' Farrington, the Government Whip, has a great deal of difficulty in maintaining a Labour majority, particularly without Liberal support.

I have been particularly grateful for the friendship of many colleagues. Among them is Stan Orme (formerly MP for Salford East, Minister for Social Security in the Cabinet 1976-79 and former Chairman of the Parliamentary Labour Party). Two Trade Union friends, who entered the Lords at the same time, are Lord (Garfield) Davies, former General Secretary of USDAW (Union of Shop, Distributive and Allied Workers) and Lord (Keith) Brookman, former General Secretary of ISTC (Iron & Steel Trades Confederation). Since the last General Election in 2001, two long-standing friends from the Commons have joined us – Lord Morris QC (Aberavon), who had a distinguished career in the Commons and is now Chancellor of the University of Wales; and Lord Barry Jones (former MP for Alyn & Deeside), a friend over many years in the Commons with whom I worked very closely when he was Shadow Secretary of State for Wales for a time during the Thatcher years.

Barry Jones was elected to the Alyn & Deeside seat in the Commons following the retirement of Eirene White who was subsequently made a Life Peer. She was a Parliamentarian of distinction and under the Wilson Government was a Minister in the Foreign Office and Chairman of the Labour Party. Our local interest in Eirene is due to her aide Howard Moore, who worked with her for many years until her recent death. Howard, like me, is a native of Pontllanfraith. The village is unusual in that in the nearby River Sirhowy valley a picturesque old water mill has been carefully preserved. In my early days the owner was known as 'Moore the Mill'. His son was a keen telegraph operator and in a little wooden hut by the mill he picked up an SOS signal from the doomed *Titanic*. This episode in 1912 was recounted on television recently by his nephew Howard Moore.

One of my concerns in the House of Lords was compensation for miners affected by 'dust' (lung disease caused by working underground). My colleague Lord Lofthouse had been concerned about this issue for a long time, having been MP for Pontefract, and I gave him what assistance I could. We had several debates on the subject and the Minister in charge, Lord Sainsbury, looked very unhappy at our interventions.

Among the contributors to these debates was my friend Lord Hardy of Wath (former MP for Wentworth), who was closely associated with the mining industry. His father had worked in the industry. The Prime Minister in turn had appointed one Minister after another to look into this issue and to ensure that the retired miners were properly recompensed. It was pathetic to see, day after day, photographs in the *South Wales Argus* of miners with severe breathing difficulties. Many of them passed away before anything could be done for them and the widows were left to take up the compensation claims. There seemed to be a shortage of consultants to verify the claims and this added to the difficulties.

I developed a pattern of having an oral Parliamentary Question on the Order Paper on a regular basis. My understanding is that large sums of money have been paid out but there is still a lot outstanding, despite the promises that have been made by successive Ministers.

I always described the Llanwern Steelworks as the cornerstone of the economy of Newport. The inception of this great works goes back to the announcement by the Prime Minister, Harold Macmillan, on 18 November 1958. He stated that Richard Thomas and Baldwin would be building a new works on a rectangle of land half a mile wide and three miles long at Llanwern. The Government had recognised the need to modernise and increase British steel production but the decision announced was very much a political compromise. What should have been one huge steel complex on a single site was divided between Ravenscraig in Scotland and Llanwern in Wales. The fact that Macmillan had Scottish forebears may have influenced him a little but the impending General Election must have played a part, with seats to be won north of the border. Our Prime Minister told us at the time that we had never had it so good! Newport, with its favourable geographical position, looked to have a good future. Nevertheless, right from the start Llanwern was not a fully integrated works and this was a great disadvantage.

The Prime Minister's announcement about the building of the new steel works was followed by a great surge of activity. The site for the works was marshland adjoining the River Severn. A kind of gold rush began, although not for gold but for shale, to form the foundation for the works. Quarries from around forty miles from Llanwern were used to provide the shale which was brought down the valleys by lorries. It was a real stampede and anyone with a lorry was in the money. The amount of shale needed was five million tons. One can picture the constant stream of lorries tearing up and down the valleys post haste. Everyone so involved was on a 'high' but sadly ten people lost their lives as a result of accidents involving the lorries. The building of the steelworks attracted workers from all over and their earnings were ploughed back into the Newport economy, making it a real boom town.

The Spencer Works as it was called (after Sir Henry Spencer who played an important part in the early days of the steel industry) began production in September 1961. After the initial boom the following years were not without trouble, though, partly due to industrial disputes and partly because even then there was the threat from cheaper steel imports. It was inevitable that these imports threatened the future of the steelworks. So the first of many redundancies came about and Newport's economy suffered accordingly.

A few years after the steelworks opened there was a further relative setback, *vis-à-vis* the Abbey Works at Port Talbot, where a massive new iron ore terminal was opened. Instead of constructing a similar facility for Llanwern, the publicly owned Steel Corporation proceeded to supply it with iron ore by rail from the new terminal at Port Talbot.

Despite these disadvantages, Llanwern, together with the

rest of the British steel industry, flourished for some years. After the austerities of the war years there was an insatiable demand for consumer goods such as cars, washing machines, refrigerators etc. which were basically made from sheet steel. Soon, though, others entered the market in competition. Germany in particular had by now recovered from its wartime devastation. Our difficulties were compounded by the strength of the pound.

Those of us who took a keen interest in Llanwern fought for the new investment to make it a fully integrated works. What was needed was a third blast furnace and the sophisticated Concast scheme. Keith Brookman (now Lord Brookman) at the time was General Secretary of the Iron & Steel Trades Confederation. This Union organised most of the workers in the industry and was in the forefront of the fight. As to the part I played, the columns of Hansard can tell their own story. The Manager of the steelworks at the time was Bill Harrison with whom I had an excellent relationship.

Despite all the investment, Llanwern steelworks was haemorrhaging. It was all part of a general decline in the manufacturing industry throughout the country and the over-production of steel in the world market. In 1999 British Steel became part of the UK-Dutch conglomerate, Corus, but the decline was relentless. In 2001 there was an announcement that Llanwern was partly to terminate its operations, leaving many workers redundant. There were also serious implications for Ebbw Vale, which finally closed down completely in July 2002, leaving the once burgeoning town desolate. 780 jobs were lost here. Situated at the top of the valley, its prospects are not good at the present time. As the *Observer* spelt out in February 2001, 'No job safe as Corus bans UK investment.'

Looking back over the years of the Llanwern steelworks I often think of Karl Marx's maxim that nothing is constant but change. On a personal note, in 1983 the Newport Labour Party held its final meeting. At that time the town was divided into two constituencies, Newport East and Newport West. To mark the occasion, I was presented with a magnificent painting of the steelworks, the work of Philip Muiren. The award was the brainchild of a long-standing member of the Labour Party in Newport, Shirley Newnham. The picture hangs in our front entrance where it is seen by our visitors.

In the early nineties Newport Borough Council put in tremendous effort to obtain permission to erect a barrage where the River Usk runs into the Severn Estuary. This area is at the heart of Newport. Successful barrages had been built in both Cardiff and Swansea and no doubt have brought wealth to the cities. The research required was costly but the Borough Council had put the money aside for the purpose and had high hopes that the scheme would go ahead. The River Severn, of which the river Usk is a tributary, has the second highest tidal 'drop' in the world, and so the large areas of mud are part of the local landscape. They do not exactly enhance what is otherwise an attractive background to the City.

There was very great disappointment in Newport when the Secretary of State for Wales, William Hague MP, turned down the proposals on environmental grounds. It was said at the time that certain land-owning interests (salmon fishing) in the River Usk valley had swayed Hague in making his decision.

When the Cardiff Bay barrage was being planned there was some opposition to the scheme on the grounds that the environment in the valley of the River Taff would be damaged. And, too, the estuary was a haven for seabirds and waders. It was decided that the marshland adjoining the site of the Llanwern steelworks should become a new nature reserve and it has quickly become established The idea was to provide a new home for the displaced birds and in this it has succeeded.

One of Newport's treasures is the Transporter Bridge, which was built in 1903 mainly to carry workers over the river

to Lysaght's steel works. It was opened in 1906. There are only
two such bridges in Britain, the other being in Middlesbrough.
This impressive bridge, with a span of 645 feet, is unusual in
that it does not support a road. Passengers and vehicles travel
on a kind of platform, which is suspended from the iron
structure overhead and moves slowly over the river. It is
known locally as the 'gondola'. In a TV programme about
Welsh bridges, Councillor Ted Travers said, 'It's the best
landmark we've got.' He recalled the times when he and his
pals used to jump off the gondola for a swim in the river. For a
number of years Newport was administered by Gwent County
Council but later it became an independent authority again and
so in a manner of speaking the bridge was 'returned' to
Newport. This was a time for celebration and we were joined
by the Labour Minister Clare Short MP. A new bridge (George
Street) has been built to handle an ever-increasing volume of
traffic over the river Usk and so the Transporter Bridge is now
a valued museum piece. It is not used for traffic but visitors are
able to walk cross the river by using the catwalk on the span. I
am proud to be President of the Friends of Newport
Transporter Bridge.

One important development has given the citizens of
Newport an added pride in their town. As part of the Golden
Jubilee celebrations in 2002, Newport was granted City status
– an honour much deserved and long overdue. Its title now is
'The City and County Borough of Newport'. It was a privilege
for me to be a member of the City Status Bid Committee.
While there was much celebrating at the time, one person must
have felt a special pleasure – Sir Harry Jones, who, as Leader of
the Council, has served Newport with distinction over many
years. And not only Newport, for his services to Local
Government extended throughout Wales and to Britain as a
whole.

In 2001 I was rushed into hospital in Cardiff for triple heart by-pass surgery during which I suffered a stroke. Two more related operations were carried out as soon as possible afterwards. I was in hospital for four months but have very little recollection of those days. Marion recalls – 'One day I was sitting at the bedside with my daughter and we were talking about the recent election of the Leader of the Conservative Party on the resignation of William Hague. A faint voice was heard from the depths of the bed – "Iain Duncan Smith."'

I have spent a lifetime in the Labour movement and my approach has tended to be that of a critical Party loyalist. From 2001 onwards, I will not be supporting Labour in Parliamentary elections. Why? For the simple reason that, as a Peer, along with lunatics and criminals, I am debarred from voting.

After nine months of convalescence at home I felt able to return to Westminster, albeit on a low-key note. Even now people come up to me in the street and ask how I enjoy retirement.

What retirement, I wonder?

Index